IMAGES
of America

THE CANEPA
SCHOOL OF DANCE

Anthony C. and Alberta J. Canepa were born to dance together. They shared their talent and knowledge with their 11 dancing children, and through the 50 years of the Canepa School of Dance, over 3,500 people have learned how to dance.

IMAGES
of America

THE CANEPA
SCHOOL OF DANCE

Jane E. Canepa

ARCADIA
PUBLISHING

Published by Arcadia Publishing
Charleston SC, Chicago IL, Portsmouth NH, San Francisco CA

Library of Congress Catalog Card Number: 2006926958

For all general information contact Arcadia Publishing at:
Telephone 843-853-2070
Fax 843-853-0044
E-mail sales@arcadiapublishing.com
For customer service and orders:
Toll-Free 1-888-313-2665

Visit us on the Internet at http://www.arcadiapublishing.com

The Dancing Canepas performed during the summer months at resorts, nightclubs, and charity fund-raisers throughout Wisconsin and particularly in Baraboo, Lake Delton, and Wisconsin Dells. Chamber of commerce statistics estimate that over three million visitors from Illinois, Wisconsin, Iowa, and Minnesota vacation annually in the area. Family members, from left to right, are (first row) Thomas, Anthony Jr., Joseph, Claire, Alberta Jr., and Diane; (second row) Christopher, Anthony Sr., James, Jane, Antoinette, Alberta Sr., and Mary.

CONTENTS

Acknowledgments   6

Introduction   7

1.   Anthony C. (Tony) and Alberta J. Canepa   9

2.   Early School Days   11

3.   Dancing through the Years—Beginnings   17

4.   Tony's Tap Tips   41

5.   Talent Shows, Recital Performances, and
         Philanthropic Roots   45

6.   Canepa Capers   51

7.   The Road to Broadway, Via Baraboo   53

8.   School Expansion—Branches   81

9.   Dancing Canepas Identified   111

10. Alberta Sr. and Alberta Jr.   125

ACKNOWLEDGMENTS

Growing up in a family of 13 gave me an appreciation for many things in life. I am grateful to my parents, Tony and Alberta Canepa, who taught by example. I am proud and honored to be their daughter. My late sister Mary was my mentor and best friend. Like my parents, she was a great teacher and one of the main reasons I have a promotion and publicity business in Chicago.

To my siblings, thanks for being you and for letting me publicize our days as the Dancing Canepas. Today we are living our lives beyond the years in Baraboo. We were able to "be what we want to" but will always share the dancing legacy provided by our parents.

I love you all very much.

To our many friends, families, supporters, and especially our students, past, present, and future, thank you! I hope your memories are good ones and that you learned something along the way. Remember to listen to Alberta Sr.—student or not—let's all "stand up straight!"

I would like to acknowledge the love, the encouragement, and the support from my son Christopher Anthony Jonsson. My sister Bertie Canepa Reifsteck provided her wit and wisdom, inspiration and cooperation for this book. My brothers Christopher J. Canepa and Thomas V. Canepa were invaluable with emotional, technical, and legal support.

Our family friend Velna June Sadler assisted with the organization of the layout and photograph identification.

A debt of gratitude goes to Jim Fuller, Laura Bennett, and the staff at Econoprint in Lake Delton for scanning the images and recital programs. Tess Kisner provided artistic assistance and applied her vast computer talents. Hollie Wendling, my intern, assisted me with photograph identification and proofreading. A special thank-you to my friend Mike Kolodny for his encouragement with this project. I extend my heartfelt thanks to each and every one of you.

Photograph credits include Millie Canepa, Art Boettcher, Harper Studios in Reedsburg, Ronald Rich, R. J. Brayer, and Dart Drake.

INTRODUCTION

This popular dance school was formed in 1955 in Baraboo after local appliance and tire store owner Anthony (Tony) Canepa Sr. tap-danced at the Sauk County Fairgrounds as the "Mystery Merchant." Upon learning his identity, friends and neighbors begged him to give their children dance lessons. Tony observed that if he taught the neighbors and friends he should also teach his own children. The handsome Tony was a dancer at the University of Wisconsin, and his svelte wife, Alberta, had taken dancing lessons from the third grade through high school. Eventually the dancing duo had 11 children of their own, and as the dancing school grew so did the formation of the Dancing Canepas. Tony Sr. passed away suddenly on August 5, 1976. Alberta Sr. passed away on July 17, 2005. She had "retired" in the early 1980s but remained active while Alberta Jr. (Bertie Canepa Reifsteck) continued operating the school locally in Baraboo and Lake Delton and organized her own school in Colorado during the winter months. Over 3,500 students have learned to dance from the Canepa family.

In 1957, the Dancing Canepas hosted a live television broadcast in Madison. The show *Canepa Capers* featured Tony as the emcee, a ballroom dance demonstration by Tony and Alberta, and dance performances by the seven Canepa "Happy Feet" children. The half-hour show featured performances by Canepa dance school students, entertainment by young musicians and singers, and a style show presented by the sponsor. A follow-along learn-at-home dance lesson was offered with select dance routines featured in an instructional book, *Tony's Tap Tips*, written by Tony Canepa. Sponsors made the forward-thinking show possible, and the dance book was sold by mail to the home viewers.

The Dancing Canepas performed in the Baraboo area, in Madison at fund-raising telethons. They made television appearances in Milwaukee, Chicago, and all around the state of Wisconsin. The family was invited to the Columbus Day and holiday family parades in Chicago and performed at McCormick Place and on Bozo's Circus. In 1970–1972, the family was named Wisconsin State Easter Seal chairmen and continued to advocate for the organization, raising funding and awareness for children who had been afflicted by polio. In May 2005, Easter Seals of Wisconsin awarded the Canepa family a lifetime service award for their 50 years of dedication to the organization and Camp Wawbeek.

Most of the dance recitals took place at the historic Al Ringling Theatre in Baraboo. The Dancing Canepas performed routines during the show and ended with a popular fast tap buck-and-wing performed to the music "Whispering." In his youth, Tony Canepa was part of a show business act that performed with a live orchestra, and he selected the 1923 tune, which was a familiar song in his family household. Canepa stated that any orchestra could play two choruses of "Whispering" and at the spur of the moment the family would be able to perform the routine. Most advanced students are taught the routine, and to date it is still an endearing ending to each and every Canepa dance recital.

Alberta Verthein grew up dancing. After high school, she auditioned and was selected to join the 1936 Revelations, a 36-member dance troupe that toured the national vaudeville circuit and performed at state fair arenas and boardwalks. Later she joined a spin-off professional dance group, pictured at left. This troupe performed for several years in nightclubs and entertainment venues in Chicago and Wisconsin area clubs. Pictured are, from left to right, (first row) Winnie Hoveler; (second row) Lorraine Lioto, Alberta Verthein, Hazel Bailey, and Audrey Hoveler; (third row) Maria Annorino.

One

ANTHONY C. (TONY) AND ALBERTA J. CANEPA

A natural showman, Anthony C. (Tony) Canepa Sr. grew up on the west side of Madison. With his four brothers, he was active in tumbling, boxing, and gymnastics. Tony learned to tap dance at the YMCA and graduated in 1936 with a business degree from the University of Wisconsin in Madison. During his college years, he was a member of the Haresfoot Club, a student theater group with a motto that "All our girls are men, yet every one's a lady." The singing and dancing troupe did not have the budget to take females, who required chaperones, on the road, so male cast donned gowns to play women's roles. Tony honed his dance promotion and public relations skills during this time.

Living on the east side of Madison, Alberta Verthein won a grade school contest as the most physically fit third grader and entered into dancing lessons from Leo Kehl School of Dance. The youngest of three, with two older brothers, Alberta enjoyed her days in dance. Her mother sewed her costumes and encouraged her daughter to dance. Alberta learned ballet, tap, and modern jazz, dancing through grade school and high school. She toured with a professional dance troupe for over two years after high school. The troupe performed in the Madison area and traveled often by train to Milwaukee, Chicago, and New York to dance in nightclubs and theaters.

Tony Canepa and Alberta Verthein were set up on a blind date and found out later that they had a common denominator in dancing. Tony was a lieutenant commander in the U.S. Navy, and at one military dance, they won a ballroom dance contest. The rest, people say, is history.

Tony and Alberta were instrumental in the dance movement in Baraboo, encouraging boys and girls to dance; tap, ballet, and ballroom were provided for anyone with a penchant for learning. As their own children became teenagers, social dancing lessons taught on Friday evening helped many shy and reserved grade and high school students learn everything from the waltz to the watusi.

The Canepa family children span 16 years, and during that time, the dancing school blossomed to 125 students a year. Alberta and Tony were known all over the area, and they formed a club for social dancing in Baraboo at the Warren Hotel and in Lake Delton at the Dell View Hotel.

CANEPA

HAPPY FEET

SCHOOL OF DANCING

Dance Recital

Benefit Camp Wawbeek Crippled Children

Baraboo High School Auditorium

Tuesday Night, May 22, 1956   7:30 P. M.

The original program from the first Canepa dance recital featured the new school logo that was designed by Harold (Hal) Hulterstrum. The Canepa family performed a tap dance to the music "Happy Feet." The stick figures in the logo represent Tony and Alberta Canepa.

The *Baraboo News Republic* ran the photograph and caption depicting the check presentation to Camp Wawbeek. Little Alberta (Bertie) Canepa, center, is sitting on the lap of Robert Peck, Camp Wawbeek chairman. Her father, Tony Canepa, is at left, and Carol Hulterstrum, event general chairman and wife of Hal Hulterstrum, is on the right.

Two

EARLY SCHOOL DAYS

Tony and Alberta were known in many circles. They were members of St. Joseph's Catholic Church, Tony was active in the Knights of Columbus, and Alberta was involved in the Ladies Altar Sodality. The Canepa children all attended St. Joseph's grade school.

As a merchant in downtown Baraboo, Tony was active in the chamber of commerce, Baraboo Merchants, and the Sauk County Fair activities. Later Tony was active with the Benevolent and Protective Order of Elks, Kiwanis Club, and Lions Club. The Baraboo Merchants also played a role in the early days and eventual formation of the Circus World Museum. The Canepa family was also linked to the Baraboo Theatre Guild, an organization that is still active today.

Local families became early supporters, including Leroy "Pete" and Joan Litscher. Active in the Future Farmers of America, 4H, and the Sauk County Fair and events, they were in the audience when Tony Canepa, wearing a U.S. Navy sailor suit, performed his merchant tap dance at the fairgrounds. As dancers, Pete and Joan encouraged boys and girls to learn to dance. The Litschers were an integral part to the success of *Canepa Capers*, the live television show hosted by the Canepas.

Members of the Baraboo Theatre Guild supported the dance school and the recitals by volunteering. Mildred (Millie) Swanson, a reporter and photographer with the *Reedsburg Times* was one such volunteer. Millie was recruited to take publicity photographs for *Tony's Tap Tips*, an instructional booklet. She drew the stick figures that depict dance moves and positions to follow in the book. Millie later married Tony's younger brother John, and they raised five children in Baraboo. Their three daughters, Sarah, Lucy, and Mary Rose, took dance lessons.

Alberta and Tony moved to a large corner home at Ash and Fifth Streets. Clara Bohn, wife of county judge Henry Bohn and the mother of Carol Hulterstrum, welcomed the family to the neighborhood. Clara told her daughter that she admired the young Alberta as she was developing her talents with the dancing school. Carol attended a planning meeting for the first dance recital and made lifelong friends in Alberta and Tony and in Baraboo Theatre Guild volunteers Mary Ann and Larry Durand from Reedsburg. She became the first recital event chairman, while husband Hal designed the school logo that is still in use today. Larry Durand served as the show announcer, while his wife, Mary Ann, played the piano accompaniment. The performance took place in the Baraboo High School auditorium on May 22, 1956, and was the first benefit for Camp Wawbeek.

PROGRAM

Accompanist—MRS. LOUIS ROMELFANGER, JR.
Narrator—MRS. H. D. HULTERSTRUM

Miss January—SUSAN THOMPSON

Sandy Chicanich	Gretta Ranum	Mary Canepa
Connie Riopell	Patty Hoppe	Antionette Canepa
Susan Hippler	Mary Befera	Terri Arndt
Terri Weiske	Kay Walkowski	Sherry Eckhardt
Mary Anne Fillhauer	Kay Heidt	Donna Clary
Patsy Meyers	Gael Hanson	Barbara Coates

Miss February—ANETTE CONWAY

Susan Befera	Kathy Senz	Janie Canepa
Joan Hembrook	Cheri Robinson	Joan Ploetz
Pamela Harwood	Mary Lynn Arndt	Mary McGonigle

Miss March—ALBERTA CANEPA AND SISTER CLAIRE

Mary Canepa	Jim Canepa	Tony Canepa
Antionette Canepa	Jane Canepa	Chris Canepa

BOB PECK—A Few Words About Camp Wawbeek

Miss April—SHERRY ROBINSON

Antionette Canepa	Gretta Ranum	Mary Befera
Kay Heidt	Patty Hoppe	Kay Wolkowski
Gael Hanson	Mary Canepa	

Miss May—ALLISON SAUEY

Annette Conway	Marilyn Koller	Rosemary Riopell
Sandy Suefzer	Barbara Miller	Joanie Ploetz
Mary Lynn Reul	Janice Carr	

Declamation—JANE HIPPLER, The Waltz by Dorothy Parker

Miss June—SANDY SEUFZER

Barbara Coates	Terri Arndt
Sherry Eckhardt	Donna Clary

Miss July—CATHY PLOETZ

Mary Canepa	Donald Sauey	Chris Canepa
Sandy Chicanich	Craig Sauey	Jim Canepa
Norman Sauey, Jr.	Wayne Sauey	Skip Dunham
Ronald Sauey	Dennis Sauey	Noble Beardsley
Gratta Ranum	Chuck McConnell	Mike McIntyre
		The Boys

Accordian selections by GEORGE BENYO

Miss August—DONNA CLARY

Sandy Chicanich	Antionette Canepa	Mary Befera
Patty Hoppe	Mary Canepa	

Miss September—MARY LOU LEHMAN

Boys and Girls

Miss October—SUSAN BEFERA

Sandy Chicanich	Sue Ott	Mary Lou Lehman
Patty Hoppe	Debbie Carr	Susan Thompson
Mary Befera	Colleen Cummings	Janie Canepa
Antionette Canepa	Mary Canepa	Allison Sauey

Organ selections by MRS. LOUIS ROMELFANGER, JR.

Miss November—COLLEEN CUMMINGS

Connie Riopell	Norman Sauey, Jr.	Mike McIntyre
Susan Hippler	Ronald Sauey	Noble Beardsley
Terri Weiske	Donald Sauey	Chris Canepa
Mary Fillhauer	Craig Sauey	Jim Canepa
Patsy Meyers	Wayne Sauey	Skip Dunham
Chuck McConnell	Dennis Sauey	

Miss December—JOANIE HEMBROOK

Gretta Ranum	Mary Befera	Gael Hanson
Kay Wolkowski	Antionette Canepa	Patty Hoppe
Kay Heidt	Mary Canepa	

COMMITTEES

Stage Properties and Hands
Tony Canepa, Chm.
Ed Sommers
Bob Meyers
Mrs. L. Clary
Mrs. Edwin Sauey

Costumes
Mrs. Tony Canepa

Tickets
Carol Hulterstrum, Chm.
Mrs. John Hoppe, Co-Chm.
Mrs. O. J. Befera
Mrs. Neil Riopell

Programs
Hal and Carol He

Make-Up
Mrs. Keith Kinds
Mrs. Norman Sa

Soliciting
Mrs. Leslie Hans
Mrs. H. Seufzer
Mrs. L. H. Ploetz

Advertising and
Dominican Sister
Carol Hulterstrun
Pictures by Les S

The Canepa dance recital programs carried advertisements from supporters of the benefit performances. The program credits the accompanist, narrator, and guest speakers.

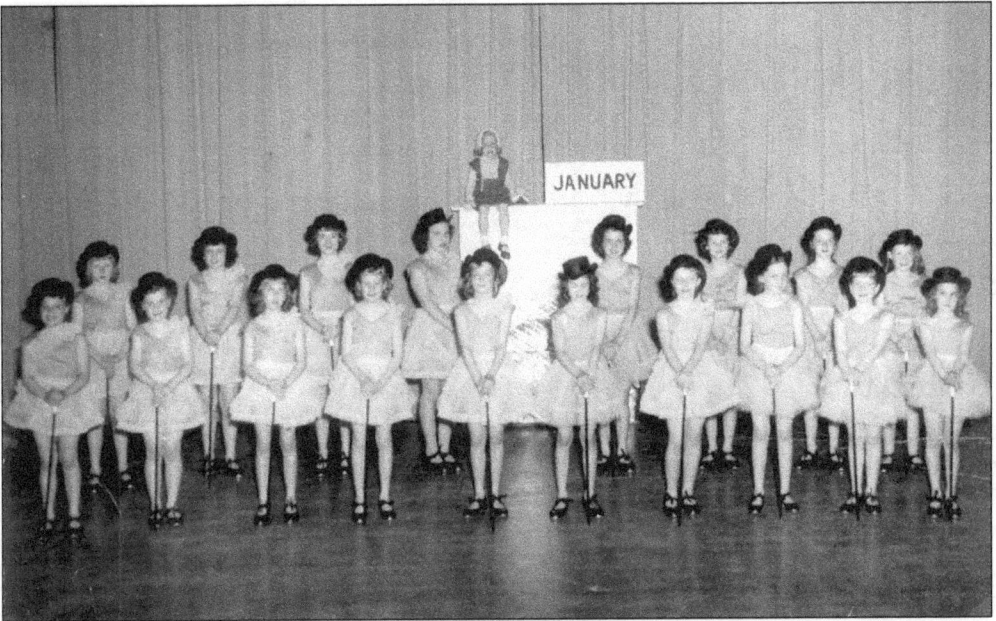

Leading the first public dance routine in the 1955 recital, a chorus line of 18 young girls from ages 9 through 12 performed a soft shoe. The dancers are, from left to right, (first row) Barbara Coates, Donna Clary, Terri Arndt, Sherri Eckhardt, Mary Anne Fillhouer, Mary Canepa, Patsy Meyers, Gael Hanson, Kay Wolkowski, and Antoinette Canepa; (second row) Susan Hippler, Terri Weiske, Sandy Chicanich, Connie Riopell, Greta Ranum, Mary Befera, Patty Hoppe, and Kay Heidt. Susan Thompson sits on the program stand to depict the month of January.

The February heartbreakers are first graders, from left to right, Jane Canepa, Kathy Sinz, Pamela Harwood, Susan Befera, Joan Hembrook, Mary Lynn Arndt, Kathy Ploetz, and Cheri Robinson. Annette Conway sits on the program stand with a huge February heart.

CANEPA
HAPPY FEET
SCHOOL OF DANCING

Dance Recital

Benefit Camp Wawbeek Crippled Children

Baraboo High School Auditorium

Tuesday Night, May 22, 1956   7:30 P. M.

Tony and Alberta Canepa organized a community-wide event with help from parents and supporters. The committees are credited in the program along with the sponsor advertising. Besides including students from the dancing school as the main performers, the Canepas presented entertainers from the area. This show featured George Benyo on the accordion and Ethel Romelfanger, the wife of Louis Romelfanger Jr., on the organ.

14

The spring Easter bonnets bring on the month of April, with Cheri Robinson in an Easter bunny suit on the program stand. Performers include, from left to right, Kay Wolkowski, Mary Canepa, Patty Hoppe, Greta Ranum, Mary Befera, Kay Heidt, Gael Hanson, and Antoinette Canepa.

Six, seven, and eight year olds are Dutch dancing maids who performed a "waltz clog" dance to welcome in the month of May. From left to right are Annette Conway, Mary Lynn Reul, Marilyn Koller, Joan Ploetz, Barbara Miller, Janice Carr, Rosemary Riopell, and Sandy Seufzer. Allison Sauey is the May flower girl.

A lineup of young men and women greets the patriotic theme with Kathy Ploetz as the Statue of Liberty. The July Fourth lineup features Cub Scouts, Boy Scouts, and a trio of patriotic ladies. From left to right are Wayne Sauey, Ronald Sauey, Donald Sauey, Christopher (Chris) Canepa, Mike McIntyre, Norman Sauey Jr., Greta Ranum, Sandy Chicanich, Mary Canepa, Skip Dunham, Noble Beardsley, Chuck McConnell, Dennis Sauey, Craig Sauey, and James (Jim) Canepa. The military fast tap dance was always a showstopper at the Canepa dance recitals.

Susan Befera, dressed as a Halloween clown, announces the four-, five-, and six-year-old tappers for the month of October. From left to right are Pamela Sauey, Allison Sauey, Debbie Carr, Kathy Ploetz, Sue Ott, Mary Lou Lehman, Jane Canepa, Colleen Cummings, Susan Thompson, Bertie Canepa, and Claire Canepa.

Three

DANCING THROUGH THE YEARS—BEGINNINGS

In the early days of the dance school, formation was through word of mouth. After Tony had performed as the Mystery Merchant in 1952 at the Sauk County Fair, he was asked to teach dancing one evening a week to neighbors' children. The Canepa School of Dance started with five youngsters and some Canepa children in the third-floor ballroom of their rambling 20-room house.

At this point, Alberta was "retired" from dancing, but Tony felt his gruff voice frightened some of the smaller pupils, and he prevailed upon her to start teaching. Tony continued to be involved in giving lessons in ballroom dancing and took on the promotion of the themed dance recitals and shows.

The Canepa children were all involved in the school from the start, enrolled in most of the classes and growing up with the school. The girls, particularly Mary and Antoinette, became teaching assistants. Many families, sisters, brothers, cousins, neighbors, and friends were eager to sign up, and although it was an expense to send students to dancing, these families were enthusiastic for the school to succeed.

Former student Laurie Litscher Siefert came to dance lessons with her brothers. They lived on a farm on Highway 33. She wrote, "What was wonderful about taking dance lessons was having the opportunity to participate in something active when there weren't many opportunities for girls—or boys for that matter—in the lower grades, especially. It also brought kids together from different schools and neighborhoods—rural and city. I think that being a part of the dance school, it made it easier when I got to junior high to feel more comfortable around the 'city' kids."

Siefert continued, "I remember walking up all those steps into that big house, feeling quite shy, but unafraid at the same time. We were always treated with patience and kindness. Even when the 'big kids' were teaching, they never took advantage of their position. It always seemed very organized. I can't imagine having that many kids milling around without producing some chaos. Alberta certainly had a magic touch dealing with children! I don't remember seeing Mr. Canepa at my lessons, but I do remember his dancing, though, with his lovely wife—what a smooth pair they made. It brings a smile to my face!"

The Canepa family residence was located at 704 Ash Street in Baraboo. The school began on the third floor in a huge ballroom space. Later the Ash Street first floor and then the Fifth Street side first floor were devoted to the school. In the 1960s, the Baraboo school was housed in the basement of the Canepa Tire and Appliance store on Fourth Street. Tony Canepa was a major influence in the initial enrollment of many boys into the school. The school focused on teaching techniques and combined some ballet with tap dancing. It was fun and provided physical fitness. Ballroom dancing was offered on Friday evenings and available to older students and adults. It was important for the youngsters of the day to become social through dancing. Dance students came from a variety of schools and adjoining towns and villages, including Baraboo, Lake Delton, North Freedom, Portage, Rock Springs, and Wisconsin Dells. Neighbors, friends, and family members, including brothers, sisters, and cousins, all took lessons. Tony produced the 1956 dance recital and the 1957 A Trip to Paris with support from Alberta and parents and community leaders. In 1958, two shows were held at the Al Ringling Theatre, with the famed Paul Luckey Orchestra on stage for Circus Days and a Christmas show that drew wide appeal in the area. The Canepas provided area youngsters with a lifetime thrill to perform on the historic Al Ringling stage. Tony and Alberta believed that every child deserved a little glamour in his life whether it was a Canepa child or a dance school student; the experience of costumes, makeup, performance excitement, socializing, and the drama of it all was fun!

18

A TRIP TO PARIS
DANCING MUSICAL REVIEW
Presented By

CANEPA

HAPPY FEE

SCHOOL OF DANCIN

BENEFIT CAMP WAWBEEK

Baraboo High School Auditori

MONDAY NIGHT, MAY 27, 1957   7:45 P. M

Seven Dancing Canepas

Summer Style Show by Herberger's

MUSIC—Mary Anne Durand—Piano
John Temte—Drums

The 1957 dance recital was themed A Trip to Paris and held at the Baraboo High School auditorium. There were seven dancing Canepa children, and the recital featured a summer-style show by Herberger's. The performers danced to live music featuring Mary Ann Durand on piano and John Temte on drums.

A TRIP TO PARIS

NARRATOR AND GUIDE - LARRY DURAND

SCENE 1, NEW YORK HARBOR

COMING ABOARD: Ensemble

ANCHORS AWEIGH: Anthony Canepa, Mary Canepa, and Gretta Ranum.

MR. ROBERT PECK, Pres. of Wisconsin Easter Seal Society

Scene 2, U. S. S. HAPPY FEET

SEMAPHORE SIGNAL CORPS: Larry Butler, Colleen Cummings, Peggy Henke and Chrissy Hill

PARASOL PROMENADE: Susan Befera, Jane Canepa, Pamela Harwood, Joan Hembrook, Mary McGonigle, Kathy Ploetz, Cheri Robinson, Allison Sauey and Kathy Sinz

HAPPY FEET: Mary Geoghegan, Julie Gibson, Mary Gruber, Mary Lou Lehman, Laurie Litscher, Mary Beth Logelin, Diane Mitchell, Sue Ott and Connie Perkins

GOBS AND MOPS: Mary Befera, Antoinette Canepa, Mary Canepa, Sandra Chicanich, Mary Anne Fillhouer, Susan Hippler, Patty Hoppe, Patty Meyers, Gretta Ranum and Teri Weiske.

WELCOME TO PARIS: Kathy Doering, Mary Jean Lewis, Scott Litscher, Sharon Murray and John Pfaff

Scene 3, STREETS OF PARIS

ARTISTS AND MODEL: Artists - Bonita Schaitel and Janet Wickus

Model - Antoinette Canepa

HOP SCOTCH: Dolly DeKeyser, Kathleen Faber, Nancy Haefer, Carol Hohn and Kathy Judson

ROPE TAP: Mary Banks, Sherrie Lee Butler, Carol Douglas, Betty Holtz, Sharon Martin, Linda Perkins and Roslyn Wick

GOVERNESSES AND BABY SITTERS: Sharon Dithmar, Barbara Miller, Mary Lee Ott, Noreen Prinz, Bonita Schaitel, Ardyth Weinke, Janet Wickus and Sandra Ziemke

BABY DOLL DANCE: Alberta Canepa, Claire Canepa, Karen Harwood, Beth Lusby, Debbie Morse and Pamela Sauey

LANNY HOWARD — Song

Scene 4, THRU THE DOOR OF CHRISTIAN DIOR

PRETTY GIRL BALLET: Mary Befera, Antoinette Canepa, Mary Canepa, Sandra Chicanich, Mary Anne Fillhouer, Susan Hippler, Patty Hoppe, Patty Meyers, Gretta Ranum, and Teri Weiske.

HERBERGER'S SUMMER STYLE SHOW: Models - Larry E Shari Dithmar, Mary Douglas, Peggy Henke, C Hill, Barbara Miller, Mary Lee Ott, John Pfaff, N Prinz, Donna Seger, Kathleen Snyder, Ardyth W and Sandra Ziemke - Narrator, Mrs. Harold Hulter

TOE AND BALLET: Mary Befera, Antoinette Canepa, Canepa, Sandra Chicanich, Candace Haferman, Hippler and Margo Nichols

CANEPA FAMILY: Monsieur et Madame Antoine Cane les enfants

Scene 5, CAFE DE' PAREE

FOLIES D' PAREE: Mary Befera, Antoinette Canepa, Canepa, Sandra Chicanich, Mary Anne Fillhouer, Hippler, Patty Hoppe, Patty Meyers, Gretta R and Teri Weiske.

MAURICE CHEVALIER AND FRIENDS: Anthony Canepa, Canepa, Michael McIntyre, Dennis Sauey and N Sauey

CAN CAN CHORUS: Susan Befera, Jane Canepa, P Harwood, Joan Hembrook, Mary McGonigle, Ploetz, Cheri Robinson, Allison Sauey and Kathy

LAWRENCE WELK AND CHAMPAIGNE LADY: Teri and Mary Fillhouer

DANCE DUO: Gretta Ranum and Mary Canepa

WAITERS: Jim Canepa, Scott Litscher, Jim Martin, Craig Donald Sauey, Ronald Sauey and Wayne Sauey

WAITRESSES: Mary Banks, Sherri Lee Butler, Carol Do Betty Holtz, Sharon Martin, Linda Perkins and I Wick

PAT AND PAT CHORUS: Featuring Patty Hoppe and Meyers. Chorus: Mary Canepa, Sandra Chicar Mary Anne Fillhouer, Susan Hippler, Gretta Ranu Teri Weiske.

Scene 6, GOING HOME

LEGIONNAIRES: Chris Canepa, Michael McIntyre, Dennis and Norman Sauey

YANKEE DOODLE DANDY - Jim Canepa

FINALE: MARSEILLES - Marche - Ensemble.

Columbia the Gem of the Ocean - Ensemble

A Trip to Paris featured every dance student performing in scenes and routines that depicted the theme of the show. The narrator and guide was Larry Durand. Community support from the Baraboo Theatre Guild, friends, and parents gave assistance to the production. Sound, lights, ticket sales, programs, scenery and props, photographs and publicity, and costumes were all part of the shows. Lorna Reul assisted Alberta Canepa with the costume creations.

In the 1957 A Trip to Paris show, Chris Canepa, who began dancing at age 11, is here at age 13 ready for his soft shoe solo.

At age eight, Jim Canepa is Yankee Doodle Dandy and ready to show his fancy footwork James Cagney style. Young Jim performed a military tap dance, putting his quick steps up and down on the specially made stairs.

The parasol promenade aboard the USS Happy Feet includes, from left to right, Jane Canepa, Allison Sauey, Kathy Sinz, Mary McGonigle, Susan Befera, Joanie Hembrook, Pamela Harwood, Kathy Ploetz, and Cheri Robinson.

The seven year olds make up the Can-Can Chorus. From left to right are (first row) Pamela Harwood, Kathy Ploetz, Allison Sauey, Jane Canepa, Cheryl Robinson, and Kathy Sinz; (second row) Susan Befera, Joanie Hembrook, and Mary McGonigle.

Hop Scotch on the Streets of Paris includes, from left to right, (first row) Dolly DeKeyser, Nancy Haefer, and Carol Henke; (second row) Kathy Judson and Kathleen Faber.

Welcome to Paris featured madams and messieurs, pictured here from left to right, John Pfaff, Sharon Murray, Kathy Doering, and Scott Litscher.

The Streets of Paris featured four, five, and six year olds. Pictured from left to right are (first row) Bertie Canepa, Claire Canepa, and Karen Harwood; (second row) Pamela Sauey, Beth Lusby, and Debbie Morse.

All aboard the USS Happy Feet sailing for Paris are the rainbow tappers. Pictured from left to right are (first row) Mary Lou Lehman, Diane Mitchell, and Sue Ott; (second row) Mary Gruber, Mary Geoghegan, Julie Gibson, Connie Perkins, and Laurie Litscher.

It is worth the wait for these lovely dancing waitresses in the Café De' Paree. Pictured from left to right are Roslyn Wick, Carol Douglas, Linda Perkins, Mary Banks, and Sherri Lee Butler.

Dancing up delightful service in the Café De' Paree are the handsome tap-dancing waiters. From left to right are (first row) Craig Sauey, Ronald Sauey, Jim Martin, and Wayne Sauey; (second row) Jim Canepa, Donald Sauey, and Scott Litscher.

The Folies De' Paree is comprised of some fancy femmes. From left to right are (first row) Sandy Chicanich, Antoinette Canepa, and Susan Hippler; (second row) Greta Ranum, Mary Befera, and Patty Hoppe; (third row) Mary Anne Fillhouer and Mary Canepa.

Maurice Chevalier had some friends that danced a stylish straw hat soft shoe. The four dapper dancers are, from left to right, Dennis Sauey, Chris Canepa, Mike McIntyre, and Norman Sauey Jr.

The streets of Paris are where two artists paint a model. Dancing through the streets from left to right are artists Janet Wickus and Bonita Schaitel, and model Antoinette Canepa.

Mary Anne Fillhouer and Terri Weiske joined other dancers for a stroll on the avenue.

The governesses waltz onto the streets of Paris. From left to right are (first row) Bonita Schaitel and Janet Wickus; (second row) Sandra Ziemke, Barbara Miller, Mary Lee Ott, and Sharon Dithmar.

The Semaphore Signal Corps aboard the USS Happy Feet are Chrissy Hill (left) and Colleen Cummings. These five year olds performed a flag-waving tap duet.

CANEPA

HAPPY FEET

SCHOOL OF DANCING

presents its

THIRD ANNUAL

CAMP WAWBEEK BENEFIT

CIRCUS DAYS

with

PAUL LUCKEY'S SAUK

COUNTY CIRCUS BAND

AL. RINGLING THEATRE

TUESDAY MAY 27, 1958   BARABOO, WISCONSIN

CIRCUS DAYS

PRODUCED AND DIRECTED BY ANTHONY AND ALBERTA CANEPA

BARABOO LAUNDRY & CLEANERS	For Plastic Costume Bags
BARABOO THEATRE GUILD	Props
BARBERSHOPPERS	Band Shell
SAUK CO. PUB. CO.	Tickets - Posters - Programs
LIONS CLUB	Clown Ushers
RED GOOSE SHOE STORE	Balloons
JOHN AND MILLIE CANEPA	Photographs - Props
JOHN KELLEY — CIRCUS WORLD MUSEUM	Back Drop - Posters
MRS. LEONE ANDERSON	Make-Up Material
DELL-PRAIRIE PRINTING CO.	Advertising
BARABOO NEWS-REPUBLIC	Advertising
FLAMBEAU PLASTICS CORP.	Use of Plastic Pails
WMTV CHANNEL 33	TV Publicity
MUSIC	Harold Hulterstrum, Adaptation Priscilla Grossman, Piano John Temte, Drums
TICKET SALES	Mrs. Peter Lacny Mrs. Arlis Perkins
COSTUMES AND DESIGNING	Alberta Canepa Lorna Reul - Marie Lovell
MAKE-UP	Lou Morse
STAGE MANAGER	Bob Meyer
ASSISTANTS	Duane Mossman - Jack Schilling Gail Butt - Ed Sommers - Randy Herfort Don Morse - Ron Campbell
SOUND	Radio Shop - John Danube

Many Thanks to all Mothers of the Youngsters in the Cast for Patience and Assistance in Helping put this Type of Show Together. Our Very Special Thanks to Paul Luckey and his Sauk County Circus Band, Priscilla Grossman, and John Temte who have Donated their Services for such a Worthy Cause.

Tony and Alberta Canepa

The Third Annual Camp Wawbeek Benefit was called Circus Days and featured a live musical performance of Paul Luckey's Sauk County Circus Band. Everyone in Baraboo got into the act, from barbershops and the Lions Club to the Circus World Museum. WMTV Channel 33 and the *Baraboo News Republic* provided publicity. Dell Prairie Printers and Sauk County Publishing Company provided tickets, posters, programs, and advertising. John Danube provided sound, Bob Meyer handled stage management, and Hal Hulterstrum provided musical adaptation along with Priscilla Grossman on piano and John Temte on drums.

Every Canepa School of Dance recital served as a fund-raiser and Robert Peck, as the representative of the Easter Seals organization, knew that young Anthony (Tony) Canepa Jr. was not clowning around with the donation. Peck addressed the audience at Circus Days, the Third Annual Camp Wawbeek Benefit, held on Tuesday, May 27, 1958, at the Al Ringling Theatre in Baraboo.

Count on a circus clown for some capers and include this fun bunch of boys. Lining up for some laughs and a fun-filled tap routine are, from left to right, Donald Sauey, Ronald Sauey, Scott Litscher, Mike McIntyre, Chris Canepa, Jim Martin, and Jim Canepa.

30

PROGRAM

JDE — Circus Tunes

TURE — Paul Luckey's Sauk County Circus Band

ATION — Mr. Robert Peck — Camp Wawbeek

HE SPEC — Grand Entree — Entire Cast

RUM MAJORETTE ....Sandy Chicanich

LOWN CAPERS ....Chris Canepa, Mike McIntyre,
Jim Martin, Ronald Sauey, Donald Sauey,
Scott Litscher, Jim Canepa

LYING HIGH ....Mary Canepa, Antoinette Canepa

IOW PONIES ....Allison Sauey, Mary Ellen
McGonigle, Mary Gruber, Susan Befera,
Pamela Harwood, Cheri Robinson, Mary Lou
Lehman, Jane Canepa, Kathy Ploetz

ABY BLUES ....Mary Jordan, Deborah K. Hoesly,
Roxy Ann Bergum, Elaine Douglas, Pamela Squires

USCLE MEN ....David Hatz, Kevin Campbell,
Jerry Litscher, John Litscher, Billy Christianson,
Dick Rathman, Freddie Pratt, Tommy Griffin

XIE PINKS ....Vicki Gerber, Karen Harwood,
Alberta Canepa, Claire Canepa, Pamela Sauey,
Barbara Hannan, Patti Thompson,
Deborah Morse, Janet Willis

APPY FEET ....Mary Frazer, Betty Holtz, Carol
Douglas, Mary Hoppe, Carolyn Myers,
Sandy Fuller, Pamela Lankey, Susan
Anstett, Jo Ann Alexander, Jean Kennedy

DY SOLDIERS ....Shirley Christianson, Mary Ann
Kieffer, Kathy Premeau, Peggy Premeau, Mary
Louise Tuttle, Mary Lynn Thompson

11. SHOOTING GALLERY.........................Chris Canepa, Mik
McIntyre, Jim Martin, Ronald Saue
Scott Litscher, Jim Canep

12. CATS ....Bonita Schaitel, Sandy Leidhold
Greta Ranum, Patsy Meyers, Mary Befer
Sandy Chicanich, Mary Canepa, Antoinette Canep

13. PRETTY BABIES ....Allison Sauey, Mary Elle
McGonigle, Mary Gruber,, Susan Befer
Pamela Harwood, Cheri Robinson, Mary Lc
Lehman, Jane Canepa, Kathy Ploe

14. TIP TOE TOT ....Alberta Canep

15. INTERMISSION — Paul Luckey's Sauk County Circus Bar

16. JOHN KELLEY — Circus World Museum

17. CLOWNING AROUND ....James Epste
Peter Greenhalgh, Paul Perkin
Bobby Brown, Michael Ban

18. PERT AND NEAT ....Bonita Schait

19. DUTCH TREAT ....Kay Cowing, Kay Zimmerma
Barbara Cummings, Nancy Alwin, Lin
Warn, Carol Ann Laubscher, Peggy L
McCoy, Sandra Warn, Bonnie Kowal

20. ON THE AVENUE ....Mary Befera, Patsy Meye

21. ON THE RESERVATION ....Cathy Doerin
Connie Perkins, Carmen Sandmire, Karen Sandmir
Ann Lovell, Ronee Gail Epstein, Gayle Kathleen Lacr
Sharon Eckhardt, Sandy Schenkat, Kathleen Fab

22. FANCY FEET ....Mary Canepa, Greta Ranu

23. THE WALTZ ....Mr. and Mrs. Tony Canep
Chris and Antoinette Canep
Jim and Jane Cane

The Dancing Canepas in 1958 featured the growing children and newest member, Joseph (Joe), holding a cane at the end of the line. The family performed together with dad and mom in many dance routines in each of the dance recitals. The children took part in many dance lessons, either in line with other students their age or helping as teaching assistants.

31

GYPSIES ....Cynthia Miller, Jolande Gumz,
Ann Arndt, Jane Jordan, Susan Powell,
Alice Marie Cook, Beth Lusby
Chaperon — Mary Douglas

SENORITA ....Mary Befera

CAPES ....Linda Wickus, Marjorie Wickus,
Fayette Johnson, Adele Allen,
Kathy O'Brien, Sharon Rathman

BULL FIGHT — Matador ....Chris Canepa,
Ferdinand the Bull — (in front) Mike McIntyre,
(in back) Scott Litscher; clown, Ronald Sauey

ZORRO .... Tony Canepa, Jr., Ronald and Donald Sauey

THE MAJORETTES ....Sharon Dithmar, Mary Lee Ott,
Sherrie Lee Butler, Dolly DeKeyser, Rosalyn Wick,
Laurie Litscher, Patricia Hohn, Mary Banks

ROPE TRICKS ....Mary Frazer, Betty Holtz,
Carol Douglas, Mary Hoppe

BLUE AND WHITE BALLET ....Bonita Schaitel, Sandy
Leidholdt, Greta Ranum, Patsy Meyers, Mary Befera,
Sandy Chicanich, Mary Canepa, Antoinette Canepa

CIRCUS ECHOES ....Paul Luckey's Band

CHEAPER BY THE DOZEN ....The Dancing Canepas

FINALE — Entire Cast

GOD BLESS AMERICA

God bless America, Land that I love, Stand beside her,
And guide her, Through the night, with the light from above
From the mountains, To the prairies, To the oceans
White with foam, God bless America, My home, sweet
home, God bless America, My home, sweet home.

DANCING CANEPAS — ANTHONY AND ALBERTA CANE

Joseph, Tony Jr., Claire, Bertie, Jane, Jimmy, Antoinette, Ma

SAUK COUNTY CIRCUS BAND
Paul Luckey, Roger Ableman, Harold Hulterstrum, William Goodn
Berger, Glen Johnson, Les Hanson, Eugene Herritz, Rollin Harding
Ed Sommers, William Hughes, Leo Parkhurst, Edwin Roeyer, Rup
David Dobson, Reedsburg; Frank Van Epps, Portage; Carl Effinge
Johnson, Madison; Morev, Pierce, Sauk City;

The performances included a variety of dancers of all ages. Paul Luckey's Sauk County Circus Band entertained before the show, at intermission, and as part of the grand finale. Attending a Canepa dance recital was a show business experience, whether a member of the cast or in the audience. Students have very positive memories of performing on the historic and storied Al Ringling stage in Baraboo.

Watching Tony and Alberta Canepa dance was a delight. They blended as a couple and were smooth as silk, especially dancing to a waltz. "Fascination" was one of their favorite songs, and joining them on stage to dance to Paul Luckey's Sauk County Circus Band are Antoinette and Chris Canepa (far left) and Jane and Jim Canepa (far right).

Paul Luckey's Sauk County Circus Band provided a fine live musical program as part of the Canepa dance recitals. Performing on the Al Ringling Theatre stage and serving as accompaniment to dancing routines, the band gave the audience a spectacular evening of entertainment. The orchestra included Baraboo members Paul Luckey (bandleader), Roger Abelman, Hal Hulterstrum, William Goodman, James Berger, Glen Johnson, Les Hanson, Eugene Herritz, and Rollin Harding. Other members were Morey Pierce, Sauk City, Carl Effinger and William Johnson, Madison, and Frank Van Epps, Portage. Ed Sommers, William Hughes, Leo Parkhurst, Edwin Roever, Rupert Werth, and David Dobson were from Reedsburg.

A packed audience enjoys the Circus Days show at the Al Ringling Theatre. A clown and a circus lion provide live entertainment as they walk through the crowds. The audience was encouraged to sing with the student performers in the grand finale. The Sauk County Circus Band played "God Bless America."

Tiny tot toy soldiers marched onto the stage in Circus Days. From left to right are Mary Lynn Thompson, Mary Ann Kieffer, Peggy Premeau, Mary Louise Tuttle, Kathy Premeau, and Shirley Christianson.

Baby girl dancers love the circus, and pictured here are, from left to right, Pamela Squires, Elaine Douglas, Roxy Ann Bergum, and Deborah K. Hoesly.

The Four Flying Femmes performed a fast tap routine. Pictured from left to right are Marjorie Wickus, Fayette Johnson, Linda Wickus, and Sharon Rathman.

Beauties on the Reservation joined in a fast tap performance. The American Indian maidens are, from left to right, (first row) Ann Lovell, Connie Perkins, Carmen Sandmire, and Karen Sandmire; (second row) Kathy Doering, Gayle Kathleen Lacny, Sandy Schenkat, Sharon Eckhardt, and Ronee Gail Epstein.

Theses 10 and 11 year olds have very happy feet. Dancing into the ring from left to right are (first row) Mary Hoppe, Pamela Lankey, Susan Anstett, and Betty Holtz; (second row) Jean Kennedy, Sandy Fuller, Mary Frazier, Carolyn Meyers, JoAnn Alexander, and Carol Douglas.

Greta Ranum and Mary Canepa are stepping high with their fancy feet footwork. The girls danced in the Circus Days recital and also performed this dance routine on the live television show *Canepas Capers*.

Hi neighbor!

Let's Get Acquainted
with

Ranum Booking Agency

of Baraboo, Wisconsin
Birthplace of "The Greatest Show on Earth"
Below are Five Steps of the Ladder to Success of the RANUM BOOKING AGENCY

MILT ☆ GREGORY ☆ GARY ☆ GRETA ☆ GORDON ☆ HELEN

RANUM BOOKING AGENCY "The Fastest Growing Agency in the Midwest"

Milt Ranum operated the Ranum Booking Agency in Baraboo. Milt and his wife, Helen, had four children. Their daughter, Greta, danced with the Canepa dance school for many years. Milt Ranum and Tony Canepa Sr. worked together on many booking engagements. The Canepa family performed at numerous chamber of commerce events in the Sauk County area and at local festivals, parades, and fairs.

ACKNOWLEDGEMENTS

RODUCER ....Anthony and Alberta Canepa

IANO ACCOMPANIMENT ....Mary Ann Durand

ET DESIGN ....Millie Canepa, Lou Morse

OSTUMES ....Alberta Canepa, Mrs. Robert Reul

AKE-UP ....Mrs. Peter Lacny

TAGE CREW ....Robert Meyer, Randall Herfort,
Donald Morse

ANTA CLAUS ....Courtesy of Baraboo Business Men's Assn.

EHEARSAL HALL ....Pine Room, Warren Hotel
Robert Buchholz, Mgr.

UBLICITY AND TICKETS ....Al. Ringling Theatre
E. J. Clumb, Mgr.

HOTO ....Rich Studio

Many thanks to all mothers of the youngsters in the cast for patience
and assistance in helping put this type of show together.
Tony and Alberta Canepa

CANEPA HAPPY FEE SCHOOL OF DANCIN

CHRISTMAS SHOW

THE DANCING CANEPA FAMILY

AL. RINGLING THEATRE
TUESDAY, DECEMBER 16, 1958 — 7:30
95 PERFORMERS
PIANO ACCOMPANIMENT ....Mary Ann

Canepa School of Dance presented a Christmas show on Tuesday, December 16, 1958, at the Al Ringling Theatre in Baraboo. A crew of set designers, stage managers, and makeup and costume assistants joined in with the production of the show. The newest addition to the Canepa lineup is nine-month-old baby Diane, holding—what else—the cane!

PROGRAM

UARY —

's Waltz ....Tony Canepa

 Wonderland ...*Kathy O'Brien, Mary Jean Lewis, Adele Allen,*
   Fayette Johnson, Patricia Neisius, Denis Hemshrot

 the Snowman ....*John Litscher, Kevin Campbell,*
   Jerry Litscher, Freddie Pratt, John Phalon

RUARY — Poster Bearer ....Kevin Campbell

heart Ballet ....*Brenda Buchholz and Antoinette Canepa*

ines ....*Jean Kennedy, Sandra Warn,*
   Peggy McCoy, Bonnie Kowalke

RCH — Poster Bearer ....Brenda Buchholz

'Canepas ....

RIL — Poster Bearer ....Tony Canepa, Jr.

Showers ....*Debbie Morse, Mary Anne Kieffer,*
   Patty Thompson, Vicki Gerber, Karen Harwood,
   Susan King, Diane Butt, Jane Jordan

Parade ....*Ruthanne Ruehlow, Karen Stowe, Marilyn Pugh*

Y — Poster Bearer ....Marilyn Pugh

lowers ....*Mistress Mary — Susan Barker, Cynthia Miller,*
   Jolande Gumz, Sheryl Gumz, Anne Arndt, Susan Powell,
   Claire Canepa, Ann Phalon, Janna Moedinger, Debbie Schacht,
   Debbie Swanson, Karen Schulenburg, Pamela Squires

Bo Peep ....*Pamela Harwood, Carol Paske, Bonnie Paske,*
   Pamela Hanson, Patti Hanson, Kim Bildsten,
   Allison Bildsten, Debbie Havener, Diane Phillips, Beth Lusby

E — Poster Bearer ....Anne Arndt

maids ....*Cheri Robinson, Mary Lou Lehman,*
   hy Ploetz, Pamela Harwood, Susan Befera, Alberta Canepa, Jr.

Party ....Bride — Jane Canepa
   Groom — John Litscher; Bestman — Jim Canepa

JULY — Poster Bearer ....Susan Befer

Glorious Fourth ....*Jim Epstein, Peter Greenhalgh*
   Laurie Litscher, Dolly DeKeyser, Rosalyn Wic

Boy on Drum ....Scott Litsche

Military Solo ....Mary Canep

AUGUST — Poster Bearer ....Peter Greenhaug

A Day at Golf ....*Greta Ranum and Sandy Chicanic*

Beauty Contest ....*Patty Doyle, Judy Doyle, Linda Goodma*
   Kathy Falk, Kathy Premeau, Kathy Steinhorst, Lenita Daviso

SEPTEMBER — Poster Bearer ....Kathy Fa

School Days — Group I ....*Jolinda Barker, Carol Laubsche*
   Rosemary Berkley, Colleen Barnhart, Linda Caflisc

Group II ....*Connie Perkins, Sharon Martin, Mary Fraze*
   Mary Hoppe, Dolly DeKeyser, Gayle Lacn
   Rosalyn Wick, Sandy Fuller, Betty Holtz, Laurie Litsche

OCTOBER — Poster Bearer ....Mary Fraze

Rah Rah Rah — Cheerleaders ....*Sandy Chicanich, Greta Ranum*
   Antoinette Canepa, Mary Canep

Football Stars ....*Scott Litcher, Jim Martin, Ronald Saue*
   Donald Sauey, Mike McIntyre
   Paul Perkins, Jim Canepa, Chris Canep

NOVEMBER — Poster Bearer ....Jim Mart

Pilgrims ....*Kay Cowing, Linda Warn, Janet Willis, Mary Jorda*

Indians ....*Cathy Doering, Jo Ann Alexande*
   Karen Sandmire, Carmen Sandmi

DECEMBER — Poster Bearer ....Karen Sandmi

SANTA CLAUS *Courtesy of Baraboo Business Men's Ass*

A Christmas Party — Clowns ....*Jim Epstein, Peter Greenhalg*
   Paul Perkins, Scott Litscher, Mike McIntyre, Donald Saue
   Ronald Sauey, Jim Martin, Jim Canepa, Chris Canep

Andy Panda ....Tony Canepa,

Ballerina Doll ....Alberta Canepa,

Harlequins ....*Greta Ranum, Mary Canepa, Antoinette Canep*
   Sandy Chicanic

Finale—Entire Cast

The Christmas show featured 95 students dancing through the year from January to December. Rehearsals for the performances were held in the Pine Room of the Warren Hotel. Tony and Alberta Canepa acknowledged the Baraboo Business Men's Association, which arranged for a guest appearance by Santa Claus, and Rich Studio handled the photography. Through the years, the Canepa family worked with a variety of merchants, including Circus City Printers, Dell Prairie Printers, and Goddard Printing, for promotional materials.

Santa Claus makes an appearance to all the performers while Tony and Alberta Canepa look on. Joe Canepa, the toddler, makes his Al Ringling stage debut.

The Christmas show finale features the entire show ensemble, including Tony and Alberta. The dancers taking center stage are, from left to right, clowns Jim Canepa, Jim Martin, Scott Litscher, Mike McIntyre, and Jim Epstein, Bertie Canepa as the ballerina, Pamela Harwood as Little Bo Peep, and her sheep. Mary Ann Durand is shown playing the piano from the orchestra pit of the Al Ringling Theatre.

Four

TONY'S TAP TIPS

Realizing that youngsters wanted to learn to dance and often many families could not afford the lessons or due to crowded scheduling they were unable, Tony Canepa penned an instruction booklet that was promoted through the television program and the school.

The booklet was prepared especially for home training in tap dancing. The Canepa School of Dance taught the five basic steps: the step, the shuffle, the hop, the brush-step, and the ball-change. Tony wrote, "As you build a home with a solid foundation—it is just as important to master the above Basic Steps before continuing on with Tap Dancing. Make sure you know the five basic steps."

The theme song of Canepa School of Dance was "Happy Feet," and the words to the song were the foundation for the *Canepas Capers* television program and for *Tony's Tap Tips*.

> Happy feet!
> I've got those happy feet!
> Give them a lowdown beat
> And they begin dancing!
> I've got those
> Ten little tapping toes,
> And when I hear a tune
> I can't control my dancing heels,
> To save my soul!
> Weary blues
> Can't get into my shoes,
> Because my shoes refuse
> To ever grow weary!
> I keep cheerful on an earful
> Of music sweet;
> 'Cause I got those happy feet la-de-da-da!

The song "Whispering" became the family theme song in later years and still is today.

> Whispering while you cuddle near me,
> Whispering so no one can hear me,
> Each little whisper seems to cheer me,
> I know its true, there's no one, dear, but you.
> Whispering why you'll never leave me,
> Whispering why you'll never grieve me,
> Whisper and say that you'll believe me,
> Whispering that I love you.

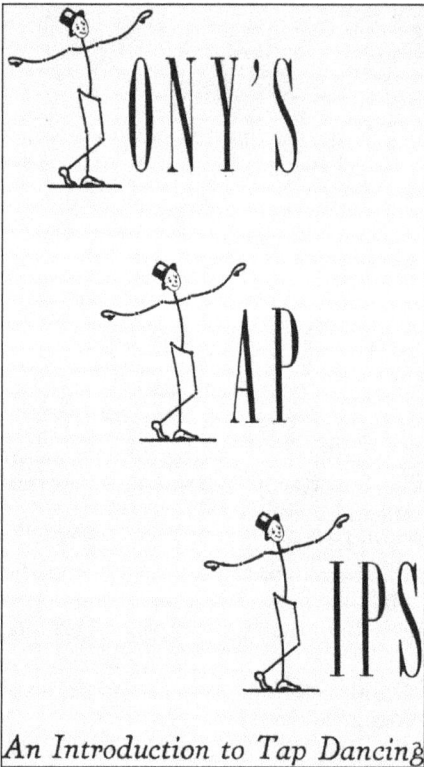

TONY'S TAP TIPS

An Introduction to Tap Dancing

Mildred Swanson was a reporter and photographer with the *Reedsburg Times Press*. She designed the dancing stick figures for the instructional pamphlet and the two editions of the *Tony's Tap Tips* book. Swanson married Tony's younger brother John, and they were active with the Baraboo Theatre Guild and the dancing school productions.

Tony Canepa was able to secure sponsorship for a complete instructional book from Redigas, a bulk gas dealer in Baraboo. The pamphlet also promoted the tap dancing show presented live on WMTV Channel 33 television in Madison. There were two versions of *Tony's Tap Tips*, and they were sold for 75¢ to $1 per copy.

Photographs of the seven Dancing Canepas were featured in the instructional book. The Canepas taught routines choreographed with musical records that could be purchased along with the book. Tony gave tap dancing tips that were easy to learn.

Seven Dancing Canepas
Claire, Alberta, Jane, Jimmy, Antoinette, Mary, Chris

ANTHONY C. CANEPA

INTRODUCTION

Tap Dancing lessons for youngsters, as a rule, can only be taken at Dancing Studios. Naturally, it is a thrill for youngsters to attend dancing school because they not only enjoy the companionship of boys and girls of the same age, but also experience a touch of the "glamor" connected with "show business". What normal child does not like to dance? Many youngsters these days find it impossible to attend dancing schools due to the over crowded schedules of working parents, lack of transportation and many other reasons.

This booklet has been prepared especially for home training in Tap Dancing.

Tap Dancing should not be limited to children only. Teenagers especially will not only have fun learning how to tap dance, but will derive great benefit as a background for social dancing. Many of the modern dance steps so popular with the high school crowd are basically tap dancing steps.

Career girls and young mothers usually find it difficult to undertake tedious exercises for body conditioning. Tap dancing for them will provide this form of exercise, and, in addition, a good deal of entertainment. So; keep trim, keep active, be graceful, learn to be a good dancer.

The Art of Tap Dancing has been broken down into its simplest form and in such a manner that the fundamentals are clearly explained. Mothers will be able to follow the instructions contained in this booklet and teach their own children. If the Mother would take a few of her child's playmates to form a class, the children will enjoy the lesson more. Taps and tap shoes for the children will add much to the effectiveness of the instruction.

How early should you start a child in Tap Dancing? Am I too heavy? Do you have to know how to dance to take up Tap Dancing? These and many other questions can be answered in a single statement. If you are able to understand instructions you will be able to Tap Dance surprisingly well. The steps contained in this booklet cover a period of about a year of class instruction. Therefore, it is not expected that the material explained here can be mastered overnight. Continued practice will show definite progress.

The Tony Canepa method of learning to dance was presented in an easy "how to tap dance" guide. Emphasizing the learning of the five basic steps and "saying the step" were the keys to the Canepa method.

43

Since Tap Dancing is primarily rhythmic it is natural that each beat of the taps must keep in time with the accompanying music. The idea presented here of "SAYING the STEP" or "SING-SONG" the steps as they are done is a great help in developing better rhythm. Have you not seen pre-kindergarten children play "Ring Around the Rosie" or "Skippety Hop to the Barber Shop." These types of games are good examples of how easily children can learn new things by "SAYING" what they are doing. Each of the Basic Steps, the Combinations of Steps and the Dance Routines contained in this booklet have been set down with the "SAYING THE STEP" idea.

This booklet is not intended as a substitute for Dancing lessons given in Dancing Schools. It's hoped that the use of this booklet will provide enjoyment for those children not able to attend Dancing Schools, and that the parents, taking the necessary time in helping their children can realize that there are few forms of exercise that will do a better job of building a straight and graceful body, developing poise and self confidence, than the art of Tap Dancing.

Included in this booklet are five simple Tap Dance Routines which are made of the Basic Steps and Combinations. Each Dance Routine requires a specific musical background and therefore the names of the tunes, length and tempo are noted opposite the pages containing the routines. The use of these recordings are recommended for home practice, and data on their availability are also noted.

FIVE BASIC STEPS

1. The Step
2. The Shuffle
3. The Hop
4. The Brush-Step
5. The Ball-Change

Note: As you build a home with a solid foundation — it is just as important to master the above Basic Steps before continuing on with Tap Dancing. Each of the Basic Steps are described in the following pages. *MAKE SURE YOU KNOW THE FIVE BASIC STEPS.*

Alberta Canepa believed that anyone at their school was capable of learning to dance; simply learning the basics, counting, and saying the step was similar to learning a language. There was pride in the fact that Canepa dancers "knew their stuff."

ROUTINES

Tap Dancing Steps set to appropriate music make up a Dance Routine. A Routine usually consists of steps so arranged as to be properly phased with the music in regard to measures and choruses. Also, Routines will vary in type among which are waltz clogs, elementary fox trot, soft shoe, fast fox trot, military, modern, eccentric and others. The degree of difficulty is also a factor in making up Routines to fit the progress shown by students. In this booklet, the Five Routines given represent over a year of progress in children's tap dancing lessons. Please note that the routines presented should be accompanied by the type of music suggested. The Russell Records as listed with each routine are available and can be purchased by submitting an order to the Canepa School of Dancing, Baraboo. Wis. The price of each record is $1.59. Add postage on all orders, 35c for single record, 05c for each additional record. Save C.O.D. charges by enclosing check or money order.

CONCLUSION

Tap dancing not only develops grace and poise but also is beneficial for children and adults as a form of exercise and recreation. For those who are interested in improving their social dancing, tap dancing provides a wonderful background in making it easier to identify various dance rhythms. The following instructions are most heartily recommended and worth your extra attention.

1. Try to Be Graceful
2. Be Light of Foot
3. Listen to the Rhythm
4. "Say" the Step
5. Keep Body Relaxed
6. Stay Off the Heels
7. HAVE FUN!

Many of the dances printed in *Tony's Tap Tips* were used to teach students. It was important that Canepa dance school students could memorize their steps, visualize the steps in classes, and practice at home. Practice and learning the steps by reading them on paper made the steps easy to learn.

Five

TALENT SHOWS, RECITAL PERFORMANCES, AND PHILANTHROPIC ROOTS

Tony and Alberta Canepa developed the groundwork for early philanthropic programs in Baraboo. Although without vast financial means, they had a talent that they shared and taught. They organized and participated in many fund-raisers. When the polio epidemic took hold of the nation, communities did their part to help fight the disease. The Canepas had a mantra, which was that they were "grateful for having 11 healthy children," and before it was fashionable or trendy, they did what they could to raise awareness and funding.

In 1957, 1958, and 1959, Tony Canepa was the general chairman of an area-wide talent show to benefit the Sauk County Chapter March of Dimes Polio Fund. Staged at the Al Ringling Theatre, the events were sponsored by the Knights of Columbus Baraboo Council No. 746. Tony assembled committees and support from advertisers, individuals, judges, merchants, volunteers, and performers, who donated their time and talent for a worthy cause.

Yearly Canepa dance recitals were also staged to benefit St. Mary's Ringling Hospital, the Circus World Museum, and Camp Wawbeek, an Easter Seal Society camp for handicapped children located in Wisconsin Dells. For a Canepa student, learning how to dance was part of attending dancing school but so was performing on a stage.

One student remembered her nervousness: being sent out on stage to perform, with glaring lights, the packed audience, and the overwhelming feeling of fear. The Canepas were used to the spotlight, and they taught their students to have confidence, "stand up straight," look out, look up, and smile. The ability to remember what one learned, keep in step with one's classmates, wear a nice costume, and hear the music made the minutes in the spotlight memorable.

Former student Laurie Litscher Siefert remembers the feelings of many dancers:

The other element was the rare opportunity to perform in front of lots of people. Dressing up in beautiful costumes—which I still have and love—and participating in a real, live production was amazing. Even though it was not a desire of mine to perform, if nothing else, it fostered a kind of confidence. Everyone started out in the fall not knowing much and then, over a few months, everyone became proficient enough to feel like something special was accomplished. I vividly remember performing on the stage in the old Baraboo High School, with the piano player down in the front, and lining up behind the curtain. It was pretty scary going out on that stage, but because we were so well prepared I don't remember any mistakes.

Sauk County Fair Board
Baraboo Theatre Guild
Baraboo Chamber of Commerce
Baraboo Men's Association
St. Mary's Ringling Hospital
St. Clare's Hospital
St. Clare Meadows
Jefferson Meadows
Ringling Brothers
Circus World Museum
Knights of Columbus
March of Dimes
Kiwanis
Lions Club
Portage Theatre Guild
Baraboo Merchants
Elks Club B.P.O.E. Fraternal Organization
University of Wisconsin – Baraboo (Boo-U)
Kids From Wisconsin
Wisconsin Singers
Milt Ranum Talent Agency
Tommy Bartlett Ski, Sky & Stage Show
Area Chambers of Commerce –
Baraboo, Reedsburg, Wisconsin Dells

In addition to Camp Wawbeek, the Easter Seal–sponsored facility in Wisconsin Dells, this is a list of organizations with which the Dancing Canepas and Canepa School of Dance were affiliated.

COMPETE IN TALENT SHOW— Over 150 Sauk county young people competed in the third annual Knights of Columbus March of Dimes Benefit Talent Show. The top picture shows the winners in each category of the junior and senior divisions. The other picture is of the entire cast during the grand finale.

The Friday, January 30, 1959, issue of the *Baraboo News Republic* featured front-page coverage of the third annual Knights of Columbus March of Dimes Benefit Talent Show. This show had winners in junior and senior divisions. Tony Canepa served as the emcee as the entire cast participated in the grand finale.

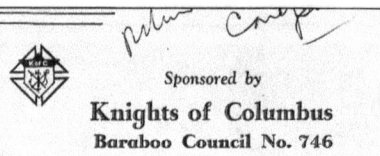

The Polio Fund Talent Show was held at the Al Ringling Theatre on Thursday, January 24, 1957. As committee general chairman, Tony Canepa pulled together a group of individuals, organizations, supporters, and performers to put on a show. The Baraboo community rallied to support the cause, and an evening of superb entertainment took place.

The entertainment lineup for the talent show drew a multitude of area entertainers. Judges were enlisted to determine the contest winners. All performers received a certificate of appreciation for their time and talent.

The Polio Fund Talent Show was repeated in 1958. Two performances were added, with a children's matinee at 3:30 p.m. and an evening program at 7:30. The committee was appreciative of the merchants who sponsored the event and who donated sufficient funds to defray the cost of the supper party for the children taking part in the show.

Over 125 performers participated in the matinee and evening performances. The Baraboo Elks Club, once a home of one of the Ringling brothers, was the site of the mid-show party.

CANEPA SCHOOL OF DANCING OFFERS:

1. Ballet
2. Tap
3. Ballroom

Call Baraboo EL 6-4663 for Details—

Have you tried these ballroom steps ? ? ?

WALTZ: Basic, Slow Turn, Open & Closed, Spin Turn, Exchange Step and Pivot
SLOW FOX TROT: Basic, Forward & Backward, Turns
CHA CHA: Basic, Open, Toe Tap, Cradle and Turns
TANGO: Basic, Cross-over, and Dip
RHUMBA: Basic, Forward and Backward, Turns and Side by Side
POLKA: Basic, Chasse and Turns

You Can Learn These in 8 Lessons!

The Dancing Canepas became known through television appearances and promotional table tents and advertising. Table tents were placed in restaurants, high-traffic areas, and tourist locations. The school recitals were also promoted through posters and recital programs. The dancing school promotions featured ballroom dancing, tap dancing, and the annual benefit recitals.

The Canepa family was well known in the tourist area of Wisconsin Dells. Photography and promotion were part of the Canepa School of Dance and the Dancing Canepas' success. Above is real-photo postcard of the family; one exception is everyone is in street clothes and not dressed alike. The postcards depicted the family members in various stages in their dancing careers and introduced new costumes and promotions for appearances and performances.

Six

CANEPA CAPERS

Canepa Capers represented another progressive idea generated by Tony Canepa. He arranged with WMTV Channel 33 to broadcast a half-hour live television program that featured the Dancing Canepas, lessons for the viewing audience, a style show, and ballroom dance instruction. Students from the dancing school were also featured, as well as youngsters with talent in music.

The 1950s brought television sets into the homes across America. Tony Canepa was in a business that sold these new machines to the consumer. Television was in its infancy along with the business of fund-raising. The pairing of the two brought the awareness of a cause and a charity to the public's eye. The live television telethon took to the airwaves, bringing area talent who volunteered their time to entertain the viewers at home.

Entertainers were recruited to fill in the hourly time slots that were broadcast live into people's homes. A television host or celebrity of the day acted as the emcee to keep the programs enlightening. Oftentimes an orchestra provided music that kept the viewers entertained. Volunteers from charities and local communities staffed the telephones, taking in pledges for the cause.

Wisconsin residents remember getting up early or staying up late to watch the Dancing Canepas perform on television. People have vivid memories of those performances. The *Wisconsin State Journal* teamed up with WISC-TV to introduce the Empty Stocking Club Christmas Charity Appeal. Phone pledges supported needy families' holiday wishes in the Madison area.

WKOW TV Channel 27 spearheaded the March of Dimes Polio Fund-raisers and involved local celebrities, entertainers, and newscasters. The late John Schermerhorn, a football hero turned television celebrity, spent one entire telethon in an iron lung. The glitz and glamour of television took over the Park Plaza Hotel in Madison for a 24-hour telethon for the March of Dimes. This provided a convention-like buzz with live cameras broadcasting from the ballroom, the entertainers staying at the hotel, and everyone rallying for a great cause. The events were electric, and Tony and Alberta Canepa were in the thick of it, and their family was asked to be part of the lineup.

Promotional flyers were created to announce the live television show produced by Tony Canepa for WMTV Channel 33 in Madison. The Dancing Canepas numbered seven children, and along with their parents, they tap-danced onto home viewers' television screens to the music of "Happy Feet." Tony and Alberta Canepa gave a ballroom dance demonstration, and students from the dancing school were invited to perform on the show. Local entertainers, including pianist Jerry Bullian, were special guests.

Sponsors were enlisted to make the television airtime possible. Gem City Dairy and Redigas were sponsors along with Herberger's, a local retail store in Baraboo that presented a style show. Tony served as the emcee and promoted his instructional book, *Tony's Tap Tips*. Tony was successful in securing a book sponsor in the Coca-Cola distributorship in Wisconsin Dells.

Seven

THE ROAD TO BROADWAY, VIA BARABOO

Canepa dance recitals were elaborately staged, with production assistance falling to Tony Canepa and dance routines and lessons handled by Alberta Canepa. As the parents of 11 children, Alberta and Tony took many cues from the U.S. Navy. Getting one child ready for a public appearance is work enough for any mother, but Alberta Canepa had a talent for keeping everyone in order and having some fun in the process.

Tony was a born promoter, using the many Ps in promotion: programs, photographs, promotional materials, and publicity. All of the Canepa children had a hand in the production. Alberta also used another talent; she sewed the Canepa family costumes and handled the design and creation, and sometimes last-minute sewing, for many of her dance students. The shows were themed, and elaborate sets were created to coincide with the specially learned dance routines. Crowds flocked to see these shows, and entertainment and enjoyment was always promised and delivered.

At Canepa School of Dance, Alberta prided herself in the fact that her students actually "learned how to dance!" The weekly classes taught basic routines, and as the year concluded, students were instructed in recital performance routines that could hold up on Broadway. Jim Halsted, a neighbor and friend, once wrote her a letter after viewing a benefit performance at the historic Al Ringling Theatre in Baraboo. He said, "Mrs. Canepa, I saw Carol Channing in Hello Dolly on Broadway, but you were better!"

1956	Dance Recital	1969	Revue 14
1957	A Trip to Paris	1970	Shufflin' Along
1958	Circus Days and Christmas Show	1971	Shall We Dance?
1959	Show Boat	1972	'72 Skidoo
1960	Hello Broadway	1973	Curtain Call '73
1961	Around the World and Parisian Holiday	1974	The Entertainers
1962	Meet Me in St. Louis	1975	Steppin' Out
1963	Summer Wonderland	1976	That's Entertainment
1964	Broadway Highlights	1977	Tap Is Back
1965	Dancing through the Year	1978	Gotta Dance
1966	Variety '66	1979	The Show Goes On
1967	Step Lively	1980	Dance, Dance and Still Dancing, 25th Anniversary Year
1968	Happy Days		

SHOW BOAT

FOURTH ANNUAL

CAMP WAWBEEK BENEFIT

MUSICAL DANCING REVUE — PRESENTED BY

CANEPA
HAPPY FEET
SCHOOL OF DANCING

THE DANCING CANEPA FAMILY PLUS
85 CHARMING STARLETS

BARABOO HIGH SCHOOL

THURSDAY, MAY 21, 1959 — 7:30 P.M.

PIANO ACCOMPANIMENT ....Mary Ann Durand

Show Boat was the theme for the 1959 Canepa dance recital. Themed dance routines were presented to a variety of songs from the musical.

A tapping duo in the Show Boat lineup was seven-year-olds Peggy McCoy (left) and Bonnie Kowalke.

54

Dancing chefs cooked up some fast tapping. Pictured from left to right are John Litscher, Glenn Goudreau, Kevin Campbell, John Phelan, and Jerry Litscher.

A tribute to Mexico with a specialty hat dance included 11- and 12-year-old girls. Pictured from left to right are (first row) Antoinette Canepa, Mary Welch, Anne Weiske, and Linda Darnell; (second row) Mary Hoppe, Kathy Platt, Jeannie Terpstra, Marilee Schuebel, and Mary Rogers.

This dancing trio includes, from left to right, Ann Phelan, Karen Schulenberg, and Pamela Squires.

Cancan dancers pictured here include, from left to right, Antoinette Canepa, Adele Allen, Mary Canepa, and Denise Hemshrot.

This lineup of six fancy dancers, from left to right, is Laurie Litscher, Sharon Martin, Mary Frazier, Mary Canepa, Rosalyn Wick, and Jane Canepa.

From left to right, sisters Carmen and Karen Sandmire dance a snappy tap routine along with JoAnn Alexander and Kathy Doering.

Sailing on the Show Boat are tiny tappers, from left to right, Susan Barker, Susan Powell, Jolande Gumz, Cynthia Miller, and Sheryl Gumz.

Petite ballerinas twirl and twinkle; from left to right are Claire Canepa, Allison Bildsten, Patti Hanson, Pamela Hanson, Debbie Havener, Diane Phillips, and Beth Lusby.

The six and seven year olds pictured here from left to right are Bertie Canepa, Karen Harwood, Vicky Gerber, Susan King, and Mary Lynn Kieffer.

From left to right, sisters Judy and Patty Doyle dance with classmates Colleen Fichter, Linda Goodman, and Kathy Steinhorst.

From left to right, Marilyn Pugh, Karen Stowe, Edith Barnhart, Linda Caflisch, and Rita Repka have fun with their kick line.

Jolinda Barker, Rosemary Berkley, Carol Laubscher, and Colleen Barnhart, from left to right, take to the stage.

Eight and nine year olds dance into the limelight. Pictured from left to right are Cheri Robinson, Kathy Ploetz, Mary Lou Lehman, Jane Canepa, Susan Befera, Pamela Harwood, and Bertie Canepa.

Ready to take the stage are, from left to right, Bertie Canepa, Debbie Morse, Cheri Robinson, Kathy Ploetz, Mary Lou Lehman, and Susan Befera.

A grand finale New Orleans style included a lineup of boys and girls. From left to right are (first row) Jerry Litscher, John Litscher, Jim Canepa, Ronald Sauey, John Phelan, and Kevin Campbell; (second row) Glenn Goodreau, Scott Litscher, Peter Greenhalgh, Mike McIntyre, Jim Epstein, Chris Canepa, and Donald Sauey.

These young girls danced with tambourines to *Show Boat* tunes. From left to right are (first row) Karen Sandmire, Laurie Litscher, Rosalyn Wick, Jolinda Barker, Bonnie Kowalke, Peggy McCoy, and Jane Canepa; (second row) Sandy Fuller, Carmen Sandmire, Antoinette Canepa, Mary Hoppe, Sharon Martin, Denise Hemshrott, JoAnn Alexander, and Colleen Barnhart; (third row) Mary Canepa, Rosemary Berkley, Kathy Doering, Carolyn Meyers, Sandy Chicanich, Mary Frazier, Carol Laubscher, Gail Lacny, and Adele Allen.

The 1960 dance recital entitled Hello Broadway was held at the Baraboo High School auditorium.

THE DANCING CANEPAS

and

CANEPA
HAPPY FEET
SCHOOL OF DANCING
PRESENT

"HELLO BROADWAY"
FIFTH ANNUAL
CAMP WAWBEEK BENEFIT
BARABOO HIGH SCHOOL AUDITORIUM
7:30 P. M. — TUESDAY, JUNE 14, 1960
PIANO ACCOMPANIMENT — MARY ANN DURAND

LITTLE DIANE CANEPA presents a $175.00 check Robert Peck for use at Camp Wawbeek. The money w raised at the fifth annual program for the camp by th Canepa School of Dance. Peck reports that Camp Wa eek is having its finest season this year.

The *Baraboo News Republic* ran a photograph and caption of a proceeds check presentation. Little Diane Canepa presents Robert Peck, Camp Wawbeek Easter Seal chairman, with a check for $175.

63

oduction and Choreography _____Anthony and Alberta Canepa

t Design _____Anthony Canepa and Mrs. John O'Malley
Lake Delton

usic _____ Mary Ann Durand

ostumes _____Alberta Canepa, Mrs. Wm. Traeder,
Mrs. W. McMahon

oeaking for Camp Wawbeek _____Bob Peck

PATRONIZE OUR HELPING HANDS

Dellview Hotel
LAKE DELTON

---

armers & Merchants
Bank
REEDSBURG

Reedsburg Bank
REEDSBURG

Baraboo National
Bank
BARABOO

Skinners Transfer
REEDSBURG

Meister & Son
REEDSBURG

Kiddie Kastle
BARABOO

Huntley Hotel
REEDSBURG

Ben's Super Market
LAKE DELTON

Clossey's
Bar & Restaurant

Wonewoc
Meat & Locker Plant

Big Store
REEDSBURG

The Square Deal Store
WONEWOC

Berning Impl. Co.
REEDSBURG

Hellpap's Little Store
WONEWOC

Gavin Agency
REEDSBURG

Schulz & Sons Variety
WONEWOC

Canepa Tire &
Retreading Co.
BARABOO

A Reedsburg - Booster

SOUTH SCHOOL — REEDSBURG
Wednesday, May 24, 1961 — 7:30 P.M.

PIANO ACCOMPANIMENT _____Mary Ann

Parisian Holiday, a Camp Wawbeek benefit, was held at South School in Reedsburg on Wednesday, May 21, 1961. Little Thomas (Tom) Canepa joined the ranks as No. 11 in the Canepa family lineup. The Canepa School of Dance had expanded to include branches in Lake Delton and Reedsburg.

64

SCENE I — OFF WE GO

OD SHIP LOLLIPOP _____Ensemble

CHORS AWEIGH _____Sharon Martin

BS AND GOBLETTES _____Susan Montgomery, Patty
Leathers, Kristine Friede, Jonelle Lassellette, Peggy
Traeder, Marjie Conlin, Joretta Marshall, Jim Held,
Patty Knuth, Gus Traeder, Lynn Gnatzig

C AND SPAN _____Janet Willis, Elaine Douglas

ISTLE A HAPPY TUNE __Debbie Horkan, Susan Montgomery,
Kerry Kate Kelly, Kristine Friede, Beth O'Malley,
Peggy Traeder, Mia Myklebust, Joretta Marshall,
Peggy Kelly, Patty Knuth, Marjie Conlin, Patty
Leathers, Jonelle Lassellette

ER THE WAVES _____Joan Connors, Mary Volk, Paula
Meister, Becky Nash, Sue Christopherson, Sandra
Walsh, Ricarda Meister, Vicki Mundth, Renee
Lassellette

ND HO! _____Casey Kelly, Jim Held, Mark Gasser,
Gus Traeder, Lynn Gnatzig

SCENE II — GAY PAREE

CEPTION _____Kristy Hanson, Susan Gruman, Ann O'Malley,
Elizabeth Dickerson, Dawn Mathews, Molly Brandt,
Mark Gasser

RLY BIRDS _____Nancy Walsh, Mark Clossey, Bonnie Schultz,
Kristy Farber, Cynthia Knight, Marcia Bodendein,
Brenda Hagan, Laura Lee Hendrickson, Peggy Kelly,
Kerry Kate Kelly, Mia Myklebust, Kent Whipp,
Beth O'Malley

SIENE _____Sue Schroeder, Karen Schullenberg,
Lynn Steinhorst

UR DE JOUR _____Laurie Fusch, Dana Marshall, Connie
Mortimer, Susan Pearson, Anne Byrne, Karen Van
Wormer, Denise Ellis, Jean Adelman, Susan Schultz,
Marcia Schultz, Kathy Held

TITE BALLET — COPPELIA _____Karen Schulenberg, Lynn
Steinhorst, Sue Schroeder, Marjie Conlin, Cynthia
Derflinger, Randi Berning, Kathy Krug, Theresa
Corwith, Llana Proper, Sandra Walsh

BES IN THE PARK _____Mark Clossey, Nancy Walsh, Brenda
Hagan, Kristy Farber, Kent Whipp, Laura Lee
Hendrickson, Marcia Bodendein, Bonnie
Schultz, Cynthia Knight

7 SHINE _____Sandy Chicanich, Sharon Mart

8 NAILA BALLET _____Betsy Knight, Sandra Braun, Sue Kell
Barbara Hasler, Mary Hasler, Connie Steiner, Dar
Marshall, Diane Walsh, Christina Tibbi

9 THE AMERICAN TOUCH _____Colleen Martin, Sharon Marti
Mary Hanson, Doreen Malisch, Mike Kelly, B
Kelly, John Dickerson, Bill Nehrir

— INTERMISSION —

SCENE III — OPERA HOUSE

Prologue to The King and I

PALACE OF THE KING OF SIAM

1 MEET THE KING AND THE ROYAL FAMILY __King—Tony Cane
Anna—Alberta Cane
Princes and Princesses—Chris, Mary, Antoinet
Jim, Jane, Alberta, Claire, Tony Jr., Joseph, Diane, To

2 CALCUTTA _____Chris and J

3 AROUND THE WORLD _____The Gi

4 BABY SCHOOL _____Joseph and Dia

5 PRINCESSES _____Mary and Antoine

6 JUNIOR GROUP _____Jane, Bertie, Claire, Tony

7 ALL TOGETHER

SCENE IV — CAFE IN PARIS

1 PEASANT DANCE _____Janet Willis, Elaine Dougl
Renee Lasselle

2 WALTZ TIME _____Colleen Martin, Sharon Martin, Mary Hanse
Doreen Malisch, Mike Kelly, Bill Kelly, Jo
Dickerson, Bill Nehr

3 MAITRE D'HOTE AND HELPERS ___Casey Kelly, Barbara Ry
Georg-Ann Stannard, Diane Schultz, Kathy Ke
Patty Parchem, Linda Hofma

4 ARTISTS AND MODELS _____Joan Connors, Mary Volk, Pa
Meister, Sue Christopherson, Ricarda Meister, Be
Nash, Sandra Walsh, Vicki Mundth, Renee Lasselle

5 CAN-CAN _____Sandy Chicanich, Sharon Mar

6 GOING HOME _____Ensem

GOD BLESS AMERICA

Students from Baraboo joined students from Reedsburg and Lake Delton to present a musical dance revue. Over 100 performers presented their best routines to piano accompaniment by Mary Ann Durand of Reedsburg. Program sponsors included the Dell View Hotel and Huntley Hotel, both locations for the Lake Delton and Reedsburg Dance Schools.

The keys to the city of Paris are presented by, from left to right, Ann O'Malley, Elizabeth Dickerson, Dawn Matthews, Susan Gruman, Molly Brandt, Kristy Hanson, and Mark Gasser.

The peasant dancers are, from left to right, Janet Willis, Renee Lassallette, and Elaine Douglas.

The Gay Paree dancing trio includes, from left to right, Sue Schroeder, Lynn Steinhorst, and Karen Schulenberg.

Early Birds catching the worm in Gay Paree are, from left to right, Mark Clossey, Kristy Farber, Cynthia Knight, Marcia Bodendein, Brenda Hagan, Laura Lee Hendrickson, Joe Canepa, Bonnie Schultz, Nancy Walsh, Mia Myklebust, Peggy Kelly, Kerry Kate Kelly, Beth O'Malley, and Kent Whipp.

The "Naila Ballet" dancers are, from left to right, Sandra Braun, Sue Kelley, Betsy Knight, Mary Hasler, Diane Walsh, Connie Steiner, Barbara Hasler, Dana Marshall, and Christina Tibbits.

The petite ballet "Coppelia" dancers from left to right are Karen Schulenberg, Marjie Conlin, Cynthia Derflinger, Kathy Krug, Sandra Walsh, Llana Proper, Theresa Corwith, Janet Willis, Lynn Steinhorst, and Sue Schroeder.

The maître d'hôtel and helpers are, from left to right, Casey Kelly, Barbara Ryan, Kathy Kelly, George-Ann Stannard, Diane Schultz, Patty Parchem, and Linda Hoffman.

Babes Dance in the Park includes, from left to right, Sandy Chicanich, Mark Clossey, Brenda Hogan, Marcia Bodendein, Laura Lee Hendrickson, Bonnie Schultz, Cynthia Knight, Kent Whipp, and Sharon Martin.

Artists and models paint a dancing palette. From left to right are Renee Lassallette, Joan Connors, Sue Christopherson, Vicki Mundth, Ricarda Meister, Paula Meister, Mary Volk, Becky Nash, and Sandra Walsh.

Sailing Away dancers from left to right are Marjie Conlin, Peggy Traeder, Patty Knuth, Lynn Gnatzig, Jim Held, Casey Kelly, Gus Traeder, Mark Gasser, Susan Montgomery, Jacqui Schmitt, Jenelle Lassallette, and Kristine Friede.

The fleur de jour ladies are, from left to right, Laurie Fusch, Dana Marshall, Connie Mortimer, Susan Pearson, Anne Byrne, Karen Van Wormer, Denise Ellis, Jean Adelman, Susan Schultz, Marcia Schultz, and Kathy Held.

Over the Waves and Off We Go includes, from left to right, Joan Connors, Renee Lassallette, Mary Volk, Paula Meister, Vicki Mundth, Sue Christopherson, Becky Nash, Sandra Walsh, and Ricarda Meister.

Whistle a Happy Tune includes, from left to right, Debbie Horkan, Mia Myklebust, Peggy Traeder, Susan Montgomery, Kerry Kate Kelly, Kristine Friede, Beth O'Malley, Joretta Marshall, Peggy Kelly, Patty Knuth, Jenelle Lassallette and Patty Leathers.

PATRONIZE OUR HELPING HANDS	
Warren Hotel	**Baraboo Bakery** Ken Hull, Mgr.
Walter Barker Mgr. J. I. Hahn Co.	**Corner Drug Store** Sylvester Budig, Prop.
A & P Walt McMahon, Mgr.	**ALPINE CAFE**
Kiddie Kastle Mr. and Mrs. Mickey Nelson	**Hill Electric Co.**
REINKING'S Fabrics of Quality	**Red Goose Shoes** for Happy Feet
Taylor's Book Store	**The Chocolate Shop**
Kerndt's Grocery	**Fisher Drugs**
Vodak Radio & T V	**HENDERSON'S** TRY OUR PIZZA
Barnhart's Badger Paint Store	**Canepa Tire & Retreading Co.**
Krueger's Barber Shop	**Hirschinger Ins.** In Baraboo Since 1922

Doing two shows in two months took great organization and strategic planning. The Canepas enlisted support from sponsors in the Reedsburg and Lake Delton communities. Joanne O'Malley, Vi McMahon, and Lorraine Traeder provided assistance with the costumes and set design. Mary Ann Durand provided the accompaniment, and Robert Peck was the guest speaker on behalf of Camp Wawbeek.

AROUND THE WORLD

HOSPITAL FUND BENEFIT

MUSICAL DANCE REVUE — PRESENTED BY

CANEPA
HAPPY FEET
SCHOOL OF DANCING

BARABOO PUPILS AND THE DANCING CANEPAS

Mon, Mary, Antoinette, Jane, Alberta, Claire, Diane,
Tommy, Joe, Tony Jr., Jim, Chris, Dad

BARABOO HIGH SCHOOL AUDITORIUM

Tuesday, June 13, 1961 — 7:30 P. M.

PIANO ACCOMPANIMENT _____Mary Ann Durand

Shown here is the Around the World Hospital Fund Benefit in the Baraboo High School auditorium, featuring Baraboo pupils and the Dancing Canepas. St. Mary's Ringling Hospital benefited from this recital. The Canepas held two shows this year, one to benefit Camp Wawbeek and the other to benefit the Baraboo hospital.

The Happy Feet dancers arriving in Calcutta are, from left to right, Bertie Canepa, Jane Canepa, Antoinette Canepa, Bonnie Kowalke, Mary Canepa, Carolyn Meyers, Rosalyn Wick, Susan Befera, Pamela Harwood, and Claire Canepa.

Sailor dancers are, from left to right, Joey Crawford, Susan Barker, Karen Harwood, JoAnn McManamy, Marilyn Pugh, Susan King, and David Larrabee.

Chinatown visitors are, from left to right, Mary Allen, Sharon Astle, Connie Smith, Darlene Miller, Darlene Ullrich, Cindy Smith, Christine Litscher, and Patsy Meyers.

"Early Bird" was a record that Alberta Canepa paid 29¢ for at Woolworth's. According to Alberta, the record was worth a million dollars in the pleasure it brought to all baby dancers. Besides learning how to dance, students learned how to count and sing, and if they could, they learned to whistle. The lyrics to "Early Bird" are as follows: "Good morning, / good morning, / nature hums the morning comes along. / Day's dawning, / stop yawning, / and begin to join me in my song. / Early bird, / up at break of day, / early bird, / sing the dark away. / Early birdies always catch a worm or two; / so don't be late you've got a date, / your worm's awaiting you. / Sleepy head / never see the sun. / Stay in bed, / always miss the fun. / Whistle in the morning. / Send the worm a warning. / Sleepy head / tumble out of bed. / Be a little early bird."

Sidewalks of New York includes, from left to right, Nancy Paschen, Carol Paske, Debbie Decker, Susan Larrabee, Jean Morse, Jill Meyers, Jana Moedinger, Cindy Lehman, and Cindy Verthein.

C'est ci Bon from Paris includes dancers, from left to right, Judy Wilson, Lynn Foley, Lindy Paschen, Carol Thiede, Pam Schilling, Bonnie Paske, Sue Dibble, Susan Major, and Pam Czys.

The baby Rockettes are, from left to right, Lisa Decker, Debbie Ryczek, Mary Schirmer, Cindy Lunde, Holly Hill, Becky Powell, and Joanie Schleicher.

The Parisian ballet includes, from left to right, Jolande Gumz, Allison Bildsten, Cynthia Miller, Carla Drake, Jane Canepa, Rosalyn Wick, an unidentified girl, Pamela Hanson, and Sheryl Gumz.

A trip to Rome and the puppet shop includes, from left to right, Patti Hanson, Janet Willis, Renee Lassallette, Elaine Douglas, Debbie Stewart, Pam Zimmerman, Claire Hirschinger, Fay Green, Wendy Schaitel, Sheri Doering, Linda Harmel, Nancy Hemshrot, Debbie King, Tony Canepa Jr. as Pinocchio, and Kim Bildsten.

A grand finale of the tarantella includes young girls from Baraboo, Reedsburg, and Wisconsin Dells.

A Trip to the Park includes, from left to right, Susan Befera, Bonnie Kowalke, Cari Hornbeck, Sherri Zimmerman, Kathy Vodak, Mary Lobaugh, Linda Wollum, Jennifer Gavin, Jane Hoppe, Carolyn Meyers, Jean Foley, and Pamela Harwood.

Striking Up the Band includes, from left to right, Susan Barker, Karen Harwood, JoAnn McManamy, Marilyn Pugh, and Susan King.

"AROUND THE WORLD"

SCENE I   EYE OPENERS

1 HAPPY FEET ____Susan Befera, Pam Harwood, Roslyn Wick, Sharon Martin, Sandy Chicanich, Carolyn
2 CALCUTTA   Myers, Bonnie Kowalke, Mary Canepa, Antoinette Canepa, Jane Canepa, Alberta Canepa, Claire Canepa

SCENE II   LONDON TOWN

1 AROUND THE WORLD _____Sharon Martin, Colleen Martin, Mary Hanson, Doreen Malisch, Bill Kelly, Mike Kelly, Bill Nehring, John Dickerson

SCENE III   PARIS

1 EARLY BIRDS _____Holly Hill, Lisa Decker, Becky Powell, Joanie Schleicher, Debbie Ryczek, Mary Shirmer, Cindy Lunde, Mark Erickson, Jennifer Gavin, Jean Foley, Kathy Vodak, Cari Hornbeck, Linda Wallum, Sherry Zimmerman, Mary Lobaugh Jane Hoppe, Pamela Miller
2 PARISIAN BALLET _____Roslyn Wick, Carla Drake, Sherrill Gumz, Jolanda Gumz, Susan Powell, Cynthia Miller, Allison Bildsten, Pam Schilling, Jane Canepa
3 C'EST CI BON _____Susan Major, Judy Wilson, Pam Czys, Carol Thiede, Lindy Paschen, Lynn Foley, Bonnie Paske, Sue Dibble, Pam Schilling
4 LA SIENE _____Lynn Steinhorst, Karen Schulenberg
5 FRERE JACQUES _____Sherry Zimmerman, Joseph Canepa
6 AT THE PARK ____Jennifer Gavin, Jean Foley, Kathy Vodak, Cari Hornbeck, Linda Wallum, Jane Hoppe, Pamela Miller Maids: Sandy Chicanich, Sharon Martin
7 CAN-CAN _____Carolyn Myers, Bonnie Kowalke

SCENE IV   ROME — PUPPET SHOP

1 FAIRY DANCE _____Kim Bildsten, Patty Hanson
2 PINOCCHIO _____Tony Canepa, Jr.
3 TARANTELLA _____Janet Willis, Elaine Douglas, Renee Lassallette
4 DOLL DANCE _____Pam Zimmerman, Debbie Stewart, Debbie King, Nancy Hemshrot, Claire Hirschinger, Fay Green, Wendy Schaitel, Linda Harmel, Sheri Doering

— INTERMISSION —

SCENE V   SIAM

Prologue to "The King and I"
PALACE OF THE KING OF SIAM

1 MEET THE KING AND THE ROYAL FAMILY King—Tony Canepa, Anna—Alberta C Princes and Princesses—Chris, Mary, Antoinette Jane, Alberta, Claire, Tony Jr., Joseph, Diane
2 SYNCOPATED CLOCK _____Top
3 BABY SCHOOL _____Bottom
4 AROUND THE WORLD BALLET_____The
5 TEA TIME _____Mom and
6 ALL TOGETHER

SCENE VI   NEW YORK

1 SIDE WALKS OF NEW YORK _____Susan Larrabee, Paske, Debbie Decker, Jill Meyers, Jana Moed Cindy Lehman, Nancy Paschen, Jean Cindy Vertein, Judy
2 CHINATOWN ____Darlene Miller, Mary Allen, Sharon Darlene Ulrich, Connie Smith, Cindy Smith, Meyers, Christine L
3 BABY ROCKETTES _____Holly Hill, Lisa Decker, Powell, Joanie Schleicher, Debbie Ryczek, Shirmer, Cindy
4 SHINE _____Susan Befera, Pam Ha
5 BROADWAY BEAT _____Sandy Chi
6 ROCK 'N' ROLL _____Coleen Martin, Sharon Mary Hanson, Dorreen Malisch, Bill Kelly, Kelly, Bill Nehring, John Dic

SCENE VII   ON THE ATLANTIC

1 ANCHORS AWEIGH ____Susan Barker, Susan King, M Pugh, Joan McManamy, Karen Ha
2 OVER THE WAVES _____David Larrabee, Joey Cro
3 SPIC & SPAN _____Janet Willis, Elaine D
4 SAILOR DANCE _____Susan Barker, Susan King, M Pugh, Joan McManamy, Karen Harwood, Larrabee, Joey Cro
5 LAND IIOI _____David Larrabee, Joey Cro

SCENE VIII   BACK HOME

1 AROUND THE WORLD ____Bonnie Kowalke, Carolyn Mary Canepa, Roslyn Wick, Antoinette C Alberta Canepa, Jane C
2 FINALE

Around the World featured dance sequences and scenes from Calcutta to Paris, Rome to Siam and Chinatown. The last scenes and grand finale always concluded with a return to the United States.

Eight

SCHOOL EXPANSION—BRANCHES

By 1962, Alberta Canepa had a schedule of teaching five days a week and an enrollment of 150 students. During the summer, they even traveled to the small town of Black Hawk one night a week to give teenagers dance lessons. Every Monday evening during the summers, the Canepa family provided entertainment as a floor show for tourists, and later in the evening, Tony and Alberta Canepa gave dance lessons to the public from 9:30 to midnight at the former Dell View Hotel in Lake Delton.

Within a few years, school branches opened in Lake Delton on Monday; Reedsburg on Tuesday; Baraboo on Thursday and Friday; and Leland, Plain, and Spring Green on Saturdays. Sundays, Wednesdays, and summer months were Alberta's days and time off. When asked what the busy mother did for fun, she stated, "golf, sew, and go out dancing with Tony one night a week."

Coordination was a common denominator in the Canepa household. There are 16 years between the oldest son, Chris, and the youngest, Tom. Chris and Mary graduated from high school in 1962 and 1963, respectively, and headed to the University of Wisconsin in Madison. During those years, Mary, like her mother, operated a dancing school and Chris, like his father, became a member of the Haresfoot Club.

As the other children followed the Canepa lineup pattern and headed to the University of Wisconsin in Madison, additional Canepa School of Dance branches sprouted. Antoinette assisted Mary with her school in Madison, and Jane formed a very successful school in Waunakee and was joined by Bertie and Claire. Diane was Alberta's full-time assistant during her grade and high school years, and she taught for a short time in Wisconsin Dells and has operated a dance school in Breckenridge, Colorado. During Jim's college days, he and Diane assisted Alberta with a school in Sauk City. Tom and Alberta ran schools in Arlington and Lodi during Tom's college days.

Tony Jr. took to the stage and performed in many community theater musicals in Indianapolis. Jane, Jim, and Bertie were in Chicago at the same time and took private lessons from the late but legendary Jimmy Payne Sr. Jim and Jane took over Payne's classes at the YMCA. Jane and Bertie go on record as being selected to be part of the first Chicago Bear cheerleader squad. Called the Bear Essentials, they were the precursor to the now defunct Honey Bears. The Canepa girls knew about dance, and they knew how to play football. After college, Bertie studied dance in Chicago with Hubbard Street, Ruth Page, Jimmy Payne Sr., and the Chicago Park District Dance Program.

"MEET ME IN ST. LOUIS"

Presented by

CANEPA
HAPPY FEET
SCHOOL OF DANCING

Dance Pupils From

Wis. Dells
Lake Delton
Reedsburg
Baraboo
Leland
Fairfield

And The Dancing Canepa Family
7th ANNUAL CAMP WAWBEEK BENEFIT

The Easter Seal Society for Crippled Children

Tues. 7:45 P.M. June 12, 1962 - Baraboo High School Auditorium

Thur. 7:45 P.M. June 14, 1962 - South School Auditorium, Reedsburg, Wis.

ADMISSION: Adults   75c   Children & Students 35c

Piano Accompanist   Mary Ann Durand

Meet Me in St. Louis featured dance pupils from Wisconsin Dells, Lake Delton, Reedsburg, Baraboo, Leland, and Fairfield. The Seventh Annual Camp Wawbeek Benefit was held on Tuesday, June 12, 1962, at the Baraboo High School auditorium and in Reedsburg on Thursday, June 14, 1962, at the South School auditorium.

ummer Wonderland Theatre - Santa Claus Town

THE DANCING CANEPA FAMILY

Joe	Jane	Tony Jr.
Mom	Mary	Chris	Diane
Antoinette	Claire	Bertie	Dad and Jim

The Dancing Canepas rode onto the stage on a bicycle built for 13. Alberta Canepa sewed the look-alike dresses for herself and her daughters. She also sewed the matching vests and sequined slacks for the boys and their father. Tony Sr. and his sons assembled the bicycle from old parts and tires from his store. The Canepas participated in a Circus Days parade in Baraboo during the summer of 1962.

Pictured in the Days in Dog Patch are, from left to right, Susan Siebert, Patty Mayer, Mary Wenban, an unidentified girl, Shirley Dewel, Debbie Morse, and Jane Kieffer.

Waiting on the levee from left to right are Tony Canepa Jr., Fritz Mellentine, David Larrabee, Kurt Litscher, Pat Eulberg, and Steven Braun.

Pictured doing a fast tap in Dog Patch are, from left to right, Lynn Steinhorst, Janet Willis, Susan Matuszek, Paula Meister, Vicki Mundt, Jean Adelman, Renee Lassallette, Ricarda Meister, and Elaine Douglas.

A dozen dancers from left to right are David Larrabee, Nancy Hemshrot, Susan Major, Patsy Meyers, Lindy Paschen, Bonnie Paske, Kristine Litscher, Carol Thiede, Fay Green, Pam Czys, Linda Harmel, and Tony Canepa Jr.

Pictured here are students from Sauk City, Leland, Plain, and Spring Green. Dancers are, from left to right, Sidney Cook, Patty Lipke, Rose Mellentine, Jacqui Wilhelm, Ann Sprecher, Bonnie Cook, an unidentified girl, Donna Jaedike, and an unidentified girl.

The dancers were able to remain on stage to watch other performances. A lineup of USS Happy Feet dancers includes, from left to right, Casey Kelly, an unidentified girl, Kathy Kelly, four unidentified dancers, Susan Befera, Jane Baryenbruch, and Susan King.

Pictured here in the Sister Ballet are, from left to right, Kim Bildsten, Pamela Hanson, Allison Bildsten, and Patti Hanson.

The costumes this summer were an Alberta Canepa brainstorm. Realizing that costumes were expensive and many siblings were in dance, she chose to order swimsuits that were trimmed with sequins. This was a great idea as the students not only had a costume, but after the recitals, they had a swimsuit. Shown here are, from left to right, Laurie Huebel, Becky Huebel, Debbie Morse, Randine Gehrke, Marsha Meister, and Marcalyn Schmitt.

Featured in Do I Hear a Waltz are, from left to right, Claire Canepa, Kathy Krug, Cynthia Derflinger, Renee Lassallette, Cynthia Knight, Bertie Canepa, and Sandra Braun.

A group of Baraboo dance pupils take to the stage. They include, from left to right, Joanie Schleicher, Jane Hoppe, three unidentified dancers, Kathy Haller, and an unidentified girl.

In June 1963, the Canepa School of Dance presented the Eighth Annual Camp Wawbeek Benefit, Summer Wonderland. There were two shows, June 11 at the Baraboo Junior High School auditorium and on June 13 in Reedsburg at the South School auditorium. Gordon Krunnfusz provided the piano accompaniment at both shows.

CANEPA HAPPY FEET SCHOOL OF DANCING

Presents

EIGHTH ANNUAL CAMP WAWBEEK BENEFIT

SUMMER WONDERLAND

Antoinette Canepa

JUNE 11, 1963, BARABOO JUNIOR HIGH SCHOOL AUDITORIUM

JUNE 13, 1963, REEDSBURG SOUTH SCHOOL AUDITORIUM

SHOWTIME 7:45

ACCOMPANIST — GORDON KRUNNFUSZ

TRY THIS ON YOUR PIANO
"Summer Wonderland"

(SEE WORDS ON OTHER SIDE)

The Summer Wonderland shows were a tribute to the Wisconsin Dells area. The chamber of commerce provided the poster backdrops, and the recitals were themed with resorts and activities in the area. A lineup of older girls opened the shows with a waltz clog dance to "School Days" and then sang and danced to the "Summer Wonderland" theme song.

89

The poster girls are, from left to right, Patti Baryenbruch, Miss River Inn; Mary Thundercloud, Miss Chula Vista; Beth Thundercloud, Miss Ishnala; Kristi Hanson, Miss Uphoff's; Lisa Gray, Miss Dellview; and Toni Thompson, Miss Devi-Bara. These young ladies took dancing from the Canepas in the Lake Delton School that was located in the Dell View Hotel.

The Fort Dells Revue includes Chris Canepa as Black Bart. Deputy assistants danced into town to help bring justice to the old fort.

The American Indian ceremonial was reenacted with a song by Debbie Day. A lineup of American Indian dancers presented an acrobatic and tap dance routine to accompany the song.

The Sugar Plum Fairy Ballet includes, from left to right, Jane Kieffer, Kim Bildsten, Patti Hanson, Bertie Canepa, Shirley Dewel, Rita Pratt, Claire Canepa, Susan Siebert, and Linda Wollum.

Corps de Ballet includes, from left to right, Diane Walsh, Cynthia Derflinger, Elaine Douglas, and Karen Schulenberg.

Corps de Ballet Part Two includes, from left to right, Marcalyn Schmitt, Kristine Friede, Cheryl Derflinger, and Jacqui Schmitt.

Delightful Dining at Fischers' Fine Foods includes, from left to right, Nancy Paschen, Jean Morse, Susan Larrabee, Diane Butt, Nancy Woelffer, and Kurt Litscher.

Jimmie's Del Bar at Your Service includes, from left to right, Suzanne Paulus, Sharon Paulus, Patricia O'Leary, Janis Kraemer, Barbara Schutz, Barbara Kraemer, Diane Kraemer, and Debbie Kraemer.

Ali Baba and the Charmers includes, from left to right, Patty Lipke, Carolee Koenig, Sidney Cook, Donna Jaedike, Jacqui Wilhelm, and Bonnie Cook.

All Aboard the Boats includes, from left to right, Vicki Kraemer, Donna Bindl, Jodi Peck, Pat Eulberg, Bruce O'Leary, Richard Umhoefer, Roxanna Galarnyk, Mary John Hutter, and Roxanna Kraemer.

Tulips, from left to right, Karen Scoles, Mary Ann Sauey, Pam Hillmer, Susan Caldwell, Morgan McArthur, and Mary Troyer are shown here.

Daisies are, from left to right, Joy Lynn Varnes, Cheri Woodbury, and Teri Jeanne Brockley.

Little tappers are ready to go. From left to right are Ellen Clossey, Emma Lee Reid, Theresa Riedel, Linda Whitney, and Diane Canepa.

Little Bo Peep and her black and white sheep are, from left to right, Kathy Coyne, Laurie Kraemer, Pam Nieder, Wendy Wiest, John Kraemer, Pat Coyne, and Patty Kraemer.

The aerialists from left to right include Laurel Huebel, Marjie Conlin, Julie Huebel, and Randine Gehrke.

Pictured here are Baraboo girls, from left to right, (seated) Linda Harmel and Nancy Hemshrot, (center) Carol Thiede; (standing) Susan Major, Kristine Litscher, and Patsy Meyers.

The Ritzy Rockettes from left to right are (first row) Mary Sue Schirmer and Debra Ryczek; (second row) Susan Nuttal, Lynn Schroeder, and Debbie King.

The Side Show Barkers and Eye Fillers from left to right are Joe Canepa, Lisa Decker, Jon Caldwell, Diane Morse, Allan Braun, Vicki Graham, Craig Caldwell, and Valerie Graham.

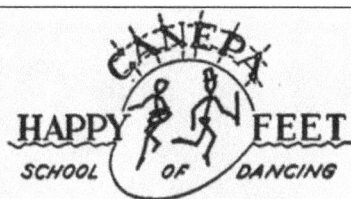

CANEPA

HAPPY FEET

SCHOOL OF DANCING

Presents

NINTH ANNUAL CAMP WAWBEEK BENEFIT

BROADWAY HIGHLIGHTS

THE DANCING CANEPA FAMILY

Baraboo Junior High School Auditorium

June 16, 1964 — Showtime 7:30 P.M.

ACCOMPANIST — MARY ANN DURAND

The Broadway Highlights recital was the Ninth Annual Camp Wawbeek Benefit, held at the Baraboo Junior High School auditorium on June 16, 1964. Many thanks were extended to the children and parents and friends who participated and supported the shows. Advertisers and sponsors helped present a multipage souvenir program book. Doug Hill, a young, talented singer, presented a variety of musical selections, including "If Ever I Would Leave You" from *Camelot*, "Tonight" from *West Side Story*, and "What Kind of Fool Am I" from *Stop the World - I Want To Get Off*. Jack Campbell, a talented musician who performed in the rotunda and piano bar at Uphoff's in Lake Delton, held a sing-along with the audience that included a variety of show tunes. A few of the selections included "Give My Regards to Broadway," "The Sidewalks of New York," and "Mary's a Grand Old Name." The words to the songs were printed in the program.

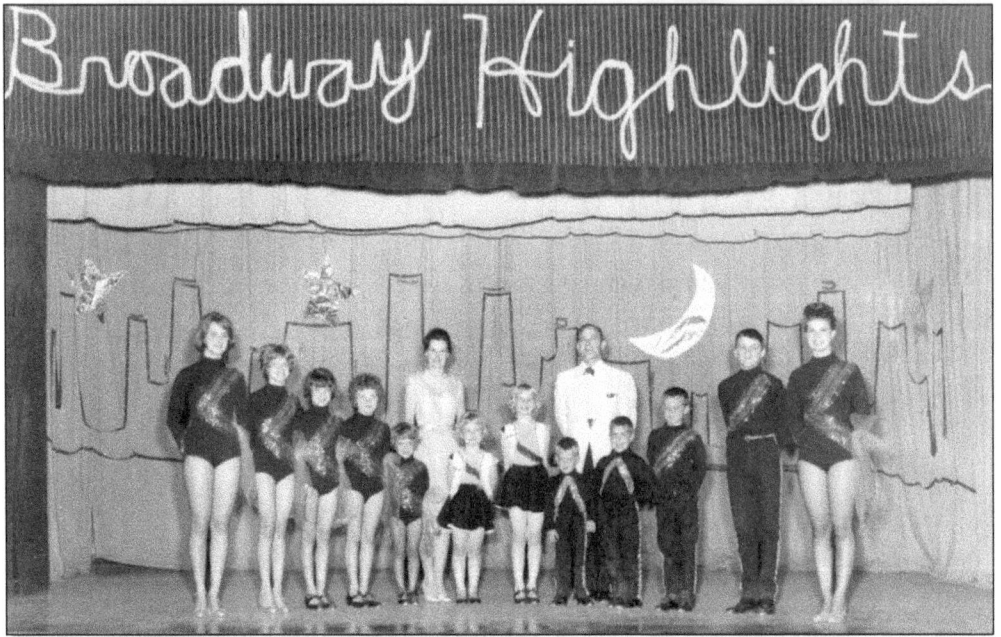

Broadway Highlights

The Dancing Canepas welcomed their audience with many specialty dance numbers within the show. The eldest son, Chris Canepa, was serving in the U.S. Navy in 1964 and missed the show. The Canepas are pictured here with Therese (left) and Christine McMahon, who performed in the *Oklahoma!* segment.

Featured in "It Don't Mean a Thing (If It Ain't Got that Swing)" are, from left to right, Susan Gruman, Patsy Meyers, Diane Walsh, Patty Kraemer, Jane Baryenbruch, Randine Gehrke, Elaine Douglas, and Marjie Conlin.

"I'm Gonna Wash that Man Right out of My Hair" from *South Pacific* features, from left to right, Patsy Meyers, Susan Gruman, Ann O'Malley, Kathy Kelly, Kristi Hanson, Susan Larrabee, Patti Baryenbruch, and David Larrabee.

"Happy Talk," from *South Pacific*, features, from left to right, Keith Lipke, Kathy Weist, Mickey Weist, Karen Kraemer, and Kay Schutz.

"Getting to Know You," from *The King and I*, features, from left to right, Machelle Drescher, Diane SaLoutos, Nancy Phillips, Holly Sonnenberg, Valerie Hegna, Gena Harms, and Dotty Roberts.

The *Irma La Duce* medley is performed by, from left to right, Marjie Conlin, Elaine Douglas, Randine Gehrke, Susan Gruman, Patsy Meyers, Diane Kraemer, Janis Kraemer, Sharon Paulus, Diane Walsh, Suzanne Paulus, Jane Baryenbruch, Barb Schutz, and Pat O'Leary.

In a hootenanny from "The Surrey with the Fringe on Top", from *Oklahoma!*, are, from left to right, Laura Herriott, Diann Johnsen, Lynnette Haskins, Mary Kay Hoffman, Cathie Ankenbrandt, and Vicki Schuebel.

"Do-Re-Mi," from *The Sound of Music*, is performed by, from left to right, Steven Braun, Paula Hoffman, Pam Hillmer, Laura Ahlstrom, Lucy Canepa, Sarah Canepa, and Butch Wolterstorff.

"Mack the Knife" is performed by, from left to right, Patty Lipke, Keith Lipke, and Debby Lipke.

"Rosie" from *Bye Bye Birdie* features, from left to right, Mary Anne Sauey, Vicky Belter, Karen Scoles, Pam Neider, Wendy Wiest, Susan Caldwell, and Diane Canepa.

"Ooh-La-La Dites Moi," from *South Pacific*, features, from left to right, Jay Neider, Nancy Owens, Merrilee Tobler, Laurie Kraemer, Linda Whitney, Julie Luke, and Tim Deininger.

The "76 Trombones" from *The Music Man*, features, from left to right, David SaLoutos, Susan Bates, Sarah Carlson, Christine McMahon, Therese McMahon, and Barbara Bates. David SaLoutos was enrolled in dancing lessons at age six. In 2003, he wrote in a birthday note to his beloved teacher: "You may never fully realize all the lives that you have touched by just being the wonderful person you are. On behalf of the hundreds of students you've taught, and the performers who have benefited from your guiding hand; I humbly say thank you. You will always be an incredible inspiration to us all."

"Hello, Dolly!" features, from left to right, Craig Caldwell, Abby Roberts, Nancy Walsh, and Jon Caldwell.

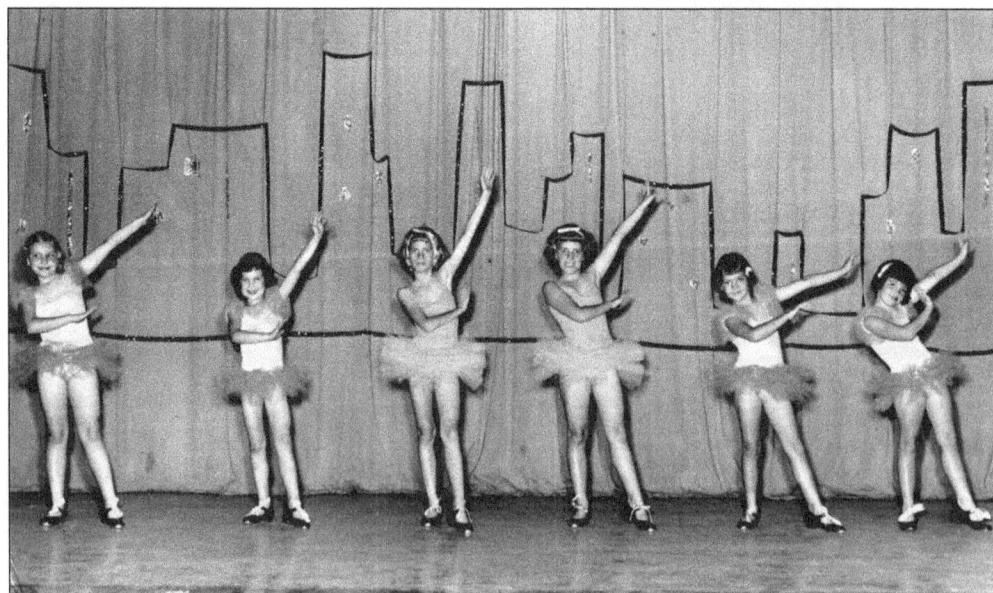

"San Francisco Here I Come" features, from left to right, Laura Lee Hendrickson, Lynn Bainbridge, Carla Schultz, Sandy Schultz, Linda Haefer, and Peggy Kelly.

"Give My Regards to Broadway" features, from left to right, Pat O'Leary, Debby Lipke, Diane Kraemer, Patty Kraemer, Sharon Paulus, Suzanne Paulus, Jane Baryenbruch, Barb Schutz, Janis Kraemer, Patty Lipke, and Jane Canepa.

Dancing through the Year was the 10th Annual Camp Wawbeek Benefit held on Tuesday, June 15, 1965, at the Baraboo Junior High School auditorium.

This group of green flower girls includes, from left to right, Carla Reinhardt, Kathleen Casey, Patti Kropp, Lisa Schultz, and Laura McArthur.

A group of blue flower girls, from left to right, Nanci Owens, Mary Ann Hanson, Amy Cone, Kim Kropp, and Lori Brockley, welcome spring.

The October Team One from left to right includes Gena Harms, Abby Roberts, Sarah Carlson, Teresa Kluender, Deanna Wolterstorff, Gayle Kiesling, Nancy Walsh, Mary Jane Slota, Kathy Morgan, Nancy Brown, and Kim Holtz.

The October Team Two from left to right includes Sue Clary, Valerie Hegna, Dottie Roberts, Peggy Belter, Ruth Ann Schuebel, Barbara Schultz, Diane Canepa, Vicki Belter, Diane SaLoutos, and Gena Harms.

The dancing dude ranchers and cowgirls are, from left to right, Merrilee Tobler, Tim Deininger, Julie Luke, Ricky Cone, Christy Mawbey, and Jay Neider.

The Nutcracker Ballet from left to right includes Raggedy Ann (Diane Canepa), Denise Wolterstorff, Bertie Canepa, Debbie Steinhorst, and Raggedy Andy (Joe Canepa).

Nine

DANCING CANEPAS IDENTIFIED

The Canepa children were expected to attend family rehearsals and to put a family dancing engagement ahead of any personal interests. Tony and Alberta Canepa sincerely hoped that dancing would be an enrichment of their children's lives rather than a profession for them. More importantly, Alberta said, "Dancing has given our children many opportunities that are hard to come by when you are one of 11 children in a family." She continued, "equally important is that they have been given an identity through dancing. They are recognized as a Dancing Canepa rather than being known as 'all those kids!'"

The early 1960s brought recital performances that included students from Baraboo, Lake Delton, Leland, Fairfield, Reedsburg, and Wisconsin Dells. The year-end recital programs were held in Baraboo one date and then Reedsburg a few days later. The Dancing Canepas had hit the road and took the students along.

The Canepa recitals were community entertainment, and along with the performances, these shows were a way to benefit a cause. The Canepas continued with the Easter Seal Society, particularly Camp Wawbeek, which provided summer respite activities for many children and young adults who were disabled. With an admission price of 35¢ for children and 75¢ for adults, sizeable donations were still raised. The Canepas found a suitable performance auditorium, enlisted the support of legions of volunteers and stagehands, managed to publish an advertisement book filled with event sponsors, and packed the house. Appreciative audiences were treated to an afternoon or evening of entertainment, and through their support, everyone's efforts were always appreciated.

Alberta was a businesswoman, and she kept a tally sheet of the monetary donations. From $176 in 1956, averages of $100, $125, $175, and even $225 for some performances were given to community organizations. These amounts in 2006 would not cover an auditorium rental.

A tribute from a friend and loyal advertising supporter appeared in the Variety '66 program. Cyril Hoffman, owner of Hoffman's Ishnala Restaurant, stated,

Dear Mr. & Mrs. Canepa, Rather than insert commercial copy on this page, we at Ishnala would like to use the space to publicly compliment you and your talented family for the abundant community interest which you have demonstrated in so many charitable forms. It has become increasingly apparent to us over the years that the Canepas are always ready and willing to dance for the benefit of any good purpose, night or day, near and far from their home. Congratulations and Thank You from all of us. Cordially, Cyril J. Hoffman, Manager.

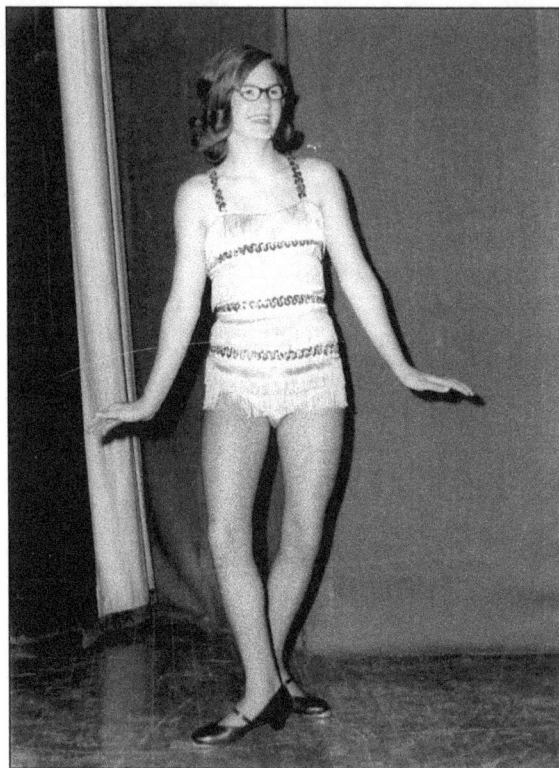

Mary Kay "Casey" Hoffman performed a solo tap dance routine. Casey danced through grade and high school. Her parents, Cyril and Velma Hoffman, supported the recitals with program advertisements, newspaper advertising, and entertainment for the dancers and families at the after-show parties. The Hoffmans owned the popular Ishnala Supper Club on Lake Delton. Clarence Zahina, a local accordionist who performed at Ishnala, often entertained. The post-recital parties were held at the Baraboo Elks Club, a former Ringling home.

This sister and brother act of fast tappers is Susan and David Larrabee.

The story of the Dancing Canepa family must include travel. They usually rode to engagements in one automobile, and after the eldest children, Chris and Mary, headed off to college, travel with the family became an art form. A request from the older college-age students to head to Florida for spring break drew a positive response from Papa Tony and Momma Alberta, "Yes, we'll all go!" The family is shown on the steps of their 704 Ash Street home and ready for a cross-country trip, which covered 1,600 miles in 10 days. Alberta and Tony took more organization tips from the U.S. Navy, and the family embarked on its first car vacation in the brand-new Oldsmobile sedan purchased from Baraboo dealer and friend Fred Kruse. The dance recitals, like the family, took on a travel theme: Variety '66 and Step Lively covered the United States through dancing.

The children and their parents were happy to head to sunny Florida. The seating arrangements were explained often as "thirteen people in one car, five in the front, and eight in the back!" Position descriptions were easy to follow, "bottom person was a base, middle person a wedge and little person, a top." Tony drove 100 miles exactly, stopping for restrooms and food and rotation, with skipping rope and Frisbee toss for exercise. Each family member was allowed one suitcase, and all other clothing, pajamas, swimsuits, and costumes were combined in fabric bags that Alberta sewed. The Dancing Canepas traveled across the state for Easter Seals, performing at numerous fund-raisers and benefits. In a Madison television studio, they taped a public service television commercial on behalf of Easter Seals for the 1971 appeal. The Canepa family is pictured here with the Easter Seals poster children, Colleen Dooley (left center) of Sheboygan and Daniel Hayes of Pardeeville.

The Girls from Uncle, from left to right, are Linda Adams, Rita Pratt, Joni Henke, Debbie Steinhorst, Mary Wenban, Susan Powell, Patti Hanson, Kim Bildsten, and Mary Louise Lobaugh.

The dancing Scoles family, pictured here from left to right, is Alan, Karen, Janet, and Linda.

Pictured here dancing at the Honeymoon Hotel in Niagara Falls are, from left to right, Tim Deininger, Annette Budig, Diane Spencer, Kathleen Casey, and Jerry Brillowski.

Pictured here along the Wabash from left to right are Debbie Candella, Shelly Rabata, Gary Brillowski, Nancy Isenberg, and Susan Rohrer.

The Parade of Stars from left to right is Denise Wolterstorff, Sarah Carlson, Marilyn Gray, Dixie Hanson, and Dawn Harwood.

The Radio City Rockettes from left to right are Diane SaLoutos, Nancy Baxter, Diane Powell, Valerie Hegna, Becky Powell, Suzanne Vodak, Teresa Kluender, Debbie Gasch, and Gena Harms.

The June Taylor Dancers from left to right are Kris Comstock, Kelly Comstock, Debbie Disch, Carolyn Green, Lori Risberg, Patty Emmerich, and Yvonne Endres. These Madison girls traveled to Baraboo to perform at the Al Ringling Theatre. The dancers took lessons from Mary Canepa's college school.

The Twelve Tappers from left to right are Tim Deininger, Mary Massong, Linda Johnson, Jeanne Madalon, Janice Swanson, Theresa Stieve, Susan Goeb, Marie May, and Bryan Schepp.

Pitter Patter Dancers are, from left to right, Connie Moe, Michelle Ofstun, Lisa Herbert, L'Rae Herbert, Kathy Ann Schultz, Rose Marie Jauch, Susan Wick, and Joni Schleicher.

The Caldwell family took dancing lessons for many years. Entertaining routines and costumes were presented by twins Craig and Jon Caldwell and sister Susan.

Friends, cousins, brothers, and sisters took dance lessons together. Jane and Patty Baryenbruch were from Wisconsin Dells. The three Roznos sisters, Bunny, Sheila, and Veronica, Robin Shale, Deanna Wolterstorff, Mary Lenzendorf, Marcia Tollaksen, and Diane, Becky, and Susan Powell also appear in the images.

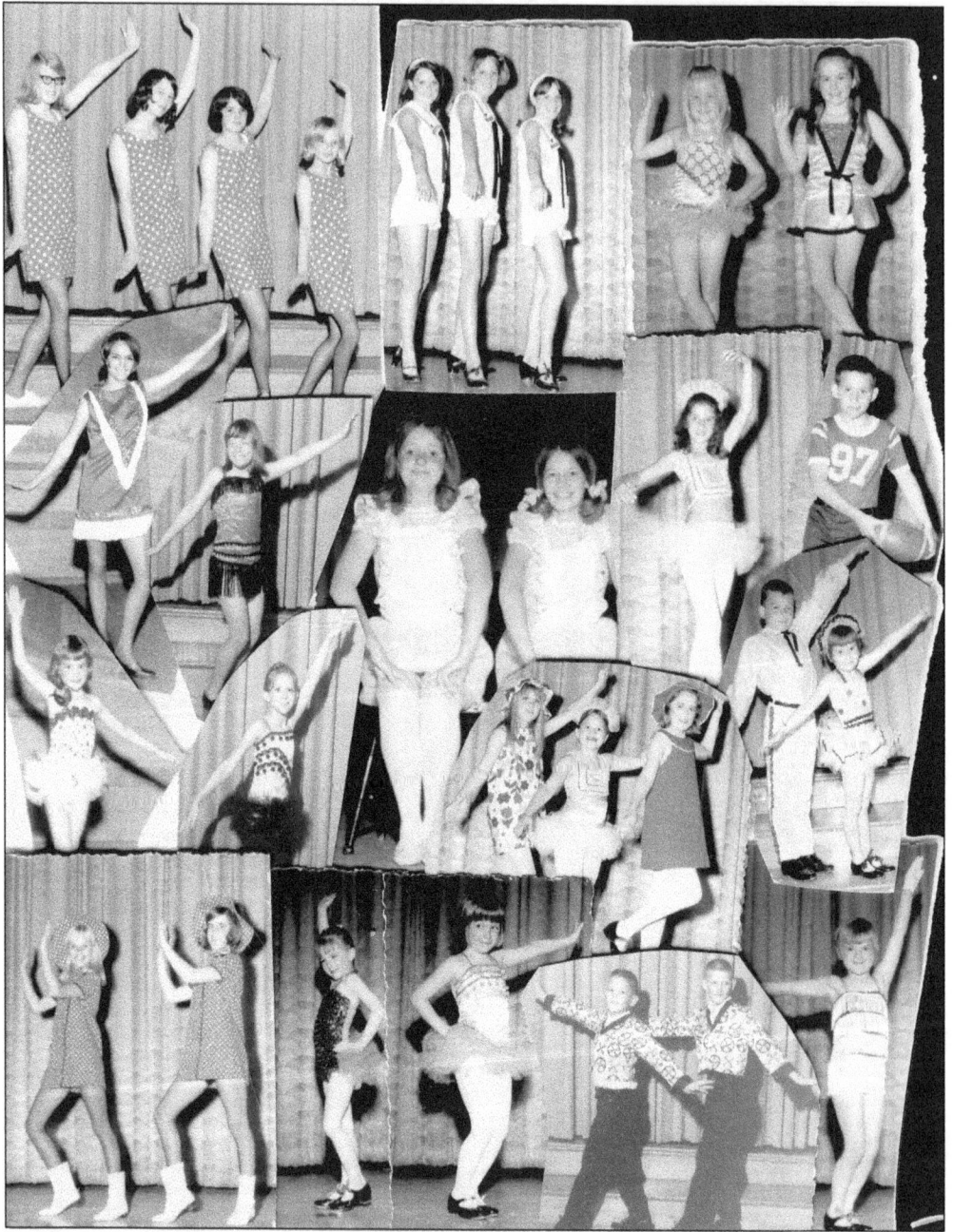

Costumes and styles of the day were always part of the Canepa dance recitals. From miniskirts, go-go boots, flapper dresses, shifts, and sailor dresses, the shows provided a fashion statement along with current music and dances.

Recital performances and costumes were a big part of the dancing school. Pictured here are four young girl dance lineups featuring a variety of costumes and hairstyles.

Students of all ages enjoyed dancing and recital performances. Dancers pictured here were featured in jazz routines, ballet, theme-song dances, and tap dance routines. Coordination of the shoes and the accessories were all part of the drama of a dance recital.

Recital productions were staged with popular musicals and trends. This lineup features the Dancing Canepas in a banjo routine and the Canepa sisters dancing on roller skates to "Roller Skate Rag." Songs from *The Music Man* featured older students who added performing and singing to the shows. An oversized car graced the stage for the finale from *Thoroughly Modern Millie*.

Tony Canepa Sr. and daughter Bertie watch a musical dance rehearsal for one of the many Baraboo Theatre Guild productions that they choreographed. The Canepas coordinated dance routines from the mid-1960s through the late 1990s. They were instrumental in the dance productions of numerous musical shows from *Anything Goes*, *Gypsy* (twice), *Hello, Dolly!*, *My Fair Lady*, *The Music Man*, *Oklahoma!*, and *South Pacific*. The late Jack Schilling, who served as director of many of these productions, remarked to his wife Avy, "I like to cast any Canepa in these shows because you tell them what to do, and they do it!" Tony and Alberta led a group of adults in a waltz routine for *My Fair Lady*, and after coordinating the dance numbers for *South Pacific*, Tony had to jump in to replace a sailor in the lineup who had fallen ill. Needless to say, he stole the show!

Alberta Canepa Sr. performed "Whispering" in Bertie's 2003 Baraboo dance recital at the Al Ringling Theatre. She is pictured here with daughter Bertie and her husband, Dennis Reifsteck, and their sons David (first row, left) and Marco. Jane Canepa (second row, left) and Antoinette Canepa Scully (right of Jane) also performed. Dennis opens many of the current Canepa School of Dance shows with his band, the Swing Crew. The show finale is Dennis's singing and playing his version of "Whispering," the Canepa family theme song and popular show finale.

124

Ten

ALBERTA SR. AND ALBERTA JR.

With the 11 children that Tony and Alberta Canepa had, the love was equally shared. When it came to dancing, however, they had their favorites. Jim Canepa has the body and the moves of a Gene Kelly–style dancer, and Alberta Jr. (Bertie) has the body and grace of a prima ballerina like Maria Tallchief. Of all of the children, Bertie, too, was born to dance. Alberta had unequivocal joy watching her daughter dance.

At age four, Bertie turned a watchful and studious eye toward her mother and mentor's dance steps and routines. She was an assistant teacher in her teenage years, and during grade school, she traveled to Madison to dance with Tibor Zana and the Madison Ballet. Zana wanted to send her to New York to join a national ballet company. Yearning to play in the summer with her brothers and sisters and friends was more to her liking than the rigors of a ballet lifestyle. During her college years and after, Bertie returned home many times and joined her mother in the dancing school. Bertie was the choreographer of the Canepa family dance routines and made certain the recital performances had a big-city presence.

Alberta passed away in July 2005, and the four performances staged in August of that year were dedicated to her memory. One student of Alberta, Susan Clary (née Powell), who brought her own daughter, Mackenzie, to Bertie's school, recalled taking dance lessons and about her teacher said, "She was very strict about posture, standing up straight, carrying yourself well. She was like a second mom. It was a really special part of our lives; my sisters and I were part of the dance program."

According to Bertie, her mother was very sharp and could always be counted on to give advice about running the businesses, even into her 80s. Following each year's recital, Bertie said she would sit down with her mother, sharing some laughs about how it went and a serious discussion of the performance. "After my dad died, my mother and I put on another 30 more years of shows. She provided her inspiration, her influence, her critique, and her smiles," Bertie said, "If she didn't have 11 children, she would be president. She was brilliant."

Alberta was a quiet strength, able to make one believe in oneself and just believe that one could do anything. This legacy is what Bertie carries on today. To the Canepa family members, children, and grandchildren, and to the generations of Canepa School of Dance students—Alberta and Tony are the ones watching now, and they smile in support.

There's no business like show business!

CANEPA
HAPPY FEET
SCHOOL OF DANCING

25TH

Annual Camp Wawbeek Benefit

Dance, Dance, and Still Dancing

Presented by Canepa School of Dance

Sunday, May 4, 1980

1:30 P.M.

Dance, Dance and Still Dancing was the theme of the 25th Annual Camp Wawbeek Benefit produced by the Canepa family. The children organized and participated in a tuxedo-clad tribute at the Al Ringling Theatre joined by and honoring Alberta Sr. and then the late Tony Canepa. The family was honored in May 2005 with a lifetime achievement award from Easter Seals of Wisconsin. The dancing legacy continues today through Bertie Canepa Reifsteck and her schools in Baraboo and Lake Delton, Wisconsin, and in Kremmling and Granby, Colorado. The performances are fund-raisers for Easter Seals and are community based with entertainment and advertising support.

126

The Dancing Canepas present an oversized check to Easter Seals. During 1971–1972, as the Wisconsin state Easter Seal chairmen, the family made performances around the state. Family members are, from left to right, Tom, Tony Sr., Alberta, Mary, Jim, Claire, Tony Jr., Bertie, Chris and Diane. Kneeling on the right side of the check are, from left to right, Jane, Antoinette, and Joe.

In 1980, the Dancing Canepas presented a 25th anniversary recital at the Al Ringling Theatre. Pictured from left to right are (first row) Tom, Tony Jr., Jim, Chris, and Joe; (second row) Claire, Bertie, Antoinette, Alberta, Diane, and Jane. Mary is missing from this photograph and was unable to attend the 25th recital as her three children had developed chicken pox. Tony Canepa Sr. passed away in August 1976, Mary passed away from breast cancer in 1988, and Alberta Sr. passed away in July 2005. Today the Canepa family members are scattered in Florida, Chicago, Colorado, Milwaukee, Lake Delton, and Wisconsin Dells. They have roots in Baraboo, and given the right opportunity, they are still able to perform "Whispering" and a few other routines when the band strikes up. Bertie Canepa Reifsteck carries on the 50-year dancing family legacy with Canepa School of Dance in Wisconsin and Colorado.

Visit us at
arcadiapublishing.com

9 781531 624538